Poetry and Crisis
in
The Age of Chaucer

UNIVERSITY OF NOTRE DAME

WARD-PHILLIPS LECTURES IN

ENGLISH LANGUAGE AND LITERATURE

Volume 4

Charles Muscatine

POETRY AND CRISIS

IN

THE AGE OF CHAUCER

Notre Dame & London
UNIVERSITY OF NOTRE DAME PRESS

Selections from Erich Auerbach, *Mimesis: The Representation of Reality in Western Literature*, translated by Willard R. Trask (copyright 1953 by Princeton University Press; Princeton Paperback, 1968), pp. 199–202, 56–57, 59–60, and 239. Reprinted by permission of Princeton University Press.

Library of Congress Catalog Card Number: 78-185409

Manufactured in the United States of America by
NAPCO Graphic Arts, Inc., Milwaukee, Wisconsin

CONTENTS

FOREWORD   vii

I   *Relevance, Poetic Style, and Cultural Crisis:*
      An Introduction   1

II   *The* Pearl *Poet: Style as Defense*   37

III   Piers Plowman: *The Poetry of Crisis*   71

IV   *Chaucer: Irony and Its Alternatives*   111

NOTES   146

INDEX   165

v

To William K. Wimsatt, Jr.

FOREWORD

The four essays in this book are in substance the Ward-Phillips lectures given under the title "Poetry and Cultural Crisis in the Age of Chaucer" in November, 1969, at the University of Notre Dame. I am grateful to the genial and learned company which sponsored the lectures, and particularly to Professor and Mrs. James E. Robinson, for their unforgettable hospitality.

The lectures are presented here with additional illustrations, with documentation (some of it more recent than that available in 1969), and with corrections and qualifications suggested by members of the original audience and by John Halverson and Larry Benson, who kindly read the lectures in manuscript. Much of the time for study and writing was provided by a grant from the National Endowment for the Humanities.

C.M.

I

RELEVANCE, POETIC STYLE, AND CULTURAL CRISIS: AN INTRODUCTION

IT IS VERY MUCH IN THE SPIRIT OF PROFESSORS WARD and Phillips, both of whom were devoted teachers of literature, that I address myself to the present topic. Proposing it, I am somewhat uneasily bringing into convergence a number of concerns that arise directly out of the problem of being a teacher of English literature in these particular times. It is perhaps a sign of the times that I can use the phrase "*problem* of being a teacher" for one of the most harmless and pleasurable occupations on earth. No teacher worth the name is without his moments of doubt and self-scrutiny. Yet recently—and particularly in the last five years—the teaching of humanities has become an authentic public "problem" recognized in international symposia and in massive studies. The central problem of the humanities is that of relevance. Are the humanities still relevant?[1] The question is always provoking, and is sometimes the occasion for either abject confessions of guilt and unworthiness; or for righteous, indignant, and closed assertion of the eternity of humanistic values. My own response falls somewhere in between. While I have not the slightest doubt of the value of what we are doing and teaching (in my case, medieval studies), I can imagine and forgive such doubts on the part of others. Students have a right (today a compulsive need) to ask what our relevance is; and in searching

1

for clear answers, I feel, we may even find some new or at least fresh values in our enterprise for ourselves.

When confronted by the question of relevance, teachers of literature have at least three main areas to defend—the moral, the aesthetic, and the historical. The moral argument is perhaps the most ready at hand, but it is not satisfactory by itself. To argue that literature "embodies perennial truths" seems self-evidently true only in regard to a handful of texts. In defending the study of any texts apart from those currently considered direct repositories of practical wisdom or of insights into the "permanent" in human nature, if we do not invoke beauty, we are usually forced toward a relativist position, that is, toward the argument from history, and we make our appeal for appreciation or toleration of the "truth" as seen by someone else at some other time and place. This historical argument is actually more palatable than the moral argument to the many students who have reason to doubt the existence of any absolute truth at all.

The case for the absolute beauty of literature would seem to be stronger. It has been said that the new student hates beauty and history with an equal passion, but I do not believe it. Beauty, like health, is not hard to justify to the young; or at least there is not as much quarreling with a line of Spenser or Milton, or a speech of Marlowe or Shakespeare, that makes your knees weak and your eyes moist. Nor is there, on a more philosophical level, much difficulty in showing the permanent "relevance" of works of great formal achievement. For even if relevance seems timebound, and forever asking "what good are these things to me here and now, in confronting these issues?"—there is a readily available sense in which the beautiful, being timeless, is always relevant.

But to argue that the stuff we deal with is relevant because it is beautiful also has something incomplete if not wrong with it. In the first place, we know that a good deal of the appreciation of beauty in art depends directly on a historical sense, on knowing what the words really mean, what conventions are being invoked, and what audience is being addressed. Again, much of what we deal with is not that beautiful —interesting though it still may be. Furthermore, if the beautiful is timeless, why turn to the beauty of a medieval poem (with all the incidental pains the appreciation will cost you) in preference to that of a modern one? Finally, are we not, in choosing the aesthetic gambit, really dodging the question? The beautiful, virtually to be defined by its disinterestedness and its transcendance of issues, hardly answers a question born of passionate concern with issues.

Relevance is most persuasively to be shown, I think, in a mutually interdependent set of values—at once moral, aesthetic, and historical. For the historical sense sharpens our appreciation of the moral and aesthetic import of literature, while the value-laden characteristics of literature give it peculiar authority as historical data. But I should like to emphasize the historical argument even further. It is as some kind of history that much literature is interesting when it is not obviously beautiful; and it is as a peculiar kind of history that a beautiful poem is read just because it is a *medieval* poem. It is as history that we value medieval culture, seeing in it partly ourselves, partly what we no longer are, partly what we might be. As humanists we cannot escape being historians. Our "utopian end," as Roy Harvey Pearce has put it, "is as full and complicated a sense of the past and present as we can contain in our critical imaginations."[2]

If that is true, then part of the problem of being (and of training) teachers of literature these days is that for the most part we are poor historians. This is because for the last generation our own training has heavily emphasized the aesthetic rather than the historical, and because as historians we have been content with the notion of having our own thing: *literary* history.

Our problem is that the age of literary analysis—the New Criticism—seems to have reached a dead end. Conceived in reaction to a simplistic, "positivistic" kind of history, it turned our attention to the text in and for itself and taught us to read poetry with the minute intensity that is now part of our standard equipment. The New Criticism taught us that the archaeological parts of scholarship—editing texts, tracing sources—were ancillary to the great act of reading and elucidating the text in and for itself; that the text's meaning was somehow hedged against historical relativism; that the literary work enjoyed a special *is*ness, a special ontological status.[3] The new-critical position, despite all it has taught us, can no longer be defended as an end in itself; it has led us quite naturally into a concern with literary texts so narrow as to merit the label "aestheticism." Turning us away from a bad kind of history, it has tended to turn us away from history itself.[4] It has not turned us away, perhaps, from *literary* history, partly because literary history is necessary to full textual study and partly because our earlier Germanic and positivistic tradition of literary-historical research still survives. Both of these motives are strengthened by a certain territorial concern that was greatly promoted by the New Criticism. To purge literary studies of the irrelevant, the unliterary, was to fence them in against biography, psychology, sociology, philosophy. This territorialism fit beautifully into the American university departmental organization and into a certain aping of the hardness and specialism of more scientific disciplines on the campus. Now it is widely manifested even among secondary-school teachers as an anxiety—in the face of French, algebra, and biology—about having one's own subject matter.

We study and teach "literary history," then. The phrase itself suggests what a poor, incomplete thing we have if we have no greater end in view. It is as if we were concerned, when we are at all concerned with man in time, with the history of legs, arms, or livers. No need to belabor the point. Our obligation is to history itself; our problem is: How can we make literary research and literary understanding contribute to the full, rich, complicated whole that is the history of our culture?

We would be, in fact, in an excellent position to contribute to cultural history if we knew more history and if we were more expert in finding the terms and categories in which literature and history connect. For no one doubts these days that history consists as much (if not more) in currents of feeling, modes of seeing, transformations of values, revolutions of sensibility —as in political, military, and economic events. And there are no better data than poems for the history of sensibility. But how do they connect?

As the New Criticism has slowly changed from a doctrinal position to an incidental technique, research-

ers and critics have struck out toward new positions—
new approaches, new emphases—but only a few of
them hold out promise for a new leverage on history.
The psychoanalytical, the structuralist, the mythical
and the exegetical approaches, despite their intrinsic
interest, seem to be alike in going away from history
rather than toward it.[5] On the other hand the propo-
nents of American Studies, as a group, seem closer to
cultural history than most of us, perhaps because their
material is presented to them in such a rich, mixed, and
immediate form. Some of them—particularly Roy Harvey Pearce, R. W. B. Lewis, John William Ward,
Henry Nash Smith, and Leo Marx—seem already to
embody the thing we are looking for, a man expertly at
home with literature who thinks and behaves like a
cultural historian. But although Marx, Smith, Pearce
and others have written provocatively about this subject, the Americanists have not developed a describable approach, and have not formed a school the rest
of us could join.[6]

Unlike the Americanists, we medievalists suffer from
a chronic lack of information. Ideally we should have
to find ways of reading history from shards and fragments, from mutilated or isolated instances. For this
purpose, one of the promising approaches is that of
stylistics. By stylistics I do not mean the interesting
commotion that has been going on recently in close
proximity to the study of structural linguistics. We are
justified in hoping that modern linguistics will sooner
or later contribute powerfully to literary studies. If
nothing else, a more accurate and refined grammar and
syntax should enable us to be more precise than ever
in the discrimination and description of verbal events
in literature. But at the present writing the new gram-

matical tools do not seem quite ready, and a linguistics of action or of performance is only barely emergent. What I mean by stylistics is simply the study of literature that pays large attention to the contribution of style (and of structure, as in the New Criticism) to meaning.[7]

Style has, of course, long been recognized as one of the key terms in which both literature and history can be understood. It is a primary tool of archaeology and of art history. We can speak of the style of a work or of a writer, and the style of a period or culture. Terms such as "Renaissance" and "Gothic" have been felt to make sense describing a single poem or a whole culture.[8] There are general but no less powerful and interesting ways in which stylistic and structural aspects of poems like *Paradise Lost* and the *Divine Comedy* confirm, fill out, and even epitomize our notion of the culture in which they were produced.

This approach owes something to the European movement called *Geistesgeschichte,* deriving from Hegel and Dilthey and reaching its peak in the Germany of the 1920s and '30s. *Geistesgeschichte* sought to explain artistic phenomena, including style, according to the "spirit of the age," and in the work of such art historians as Heinrich Wölfflin, Wilhelm Worringer, and Max Dvořák it produced some of our most powerful notions of period style and of the historical alternations of style. It was not so successful in literary studies, and it has latterly, in general, been discredited for its impressionism and its unrealistic assumption that ages or cultures are homogeneous wholes wherein all the artistic symptoms can be expected to fall into the same configuration. *Geistesgeschichte* was rather easily dismissed, if considered at all, by the New Criticism.[9]

Modern literary stylistics, by contrast, incorporates the New Criticism; it can utilize all we know of literary analysis. If the New Criticism (or beyond the Atlantic the tradition of *explication des textes*) had been developed in the service of cultural history, this is surely one of the ways it would have had to be used. In paying attention to poetic style on a new-critical level of intensity, literary stylistics seems to offer an answer to the charge of vagueness that eventually discredited its predecessor. For stylistic analysis can describe a text, from its syntax and imagery through its narrative form and total structure (not to speak of many other possible stylistic categories), with a new precision and concreteness. Furthermore, the stylistics of an Auerbach or a Spitzer, starting from the text rather than from the culture, or at least paying profound initial attention to the claims of the text in itself, is not bound, as *Geistesgeschichte* tended to be, to find in the work of art merely confirmation of dominant tendencies in the culture. Stylistics is attuned as well to the variant and dissident as to the conventional note. Its emphasis on the nondiscursive elements of meaning, its attempt to penetrate through the area of what the words say to what the style says, indeed, sometimes leads us to intimations of meaning unbeknownst to or repressed by the artists themselves. I am not sure that I accept fully Auerbach's reading of Dante's *Commedia,* but even the suggestions leading from his analysis of the meaning of the style of the Farinata-Cavalcante passage open exciting prospects for literature as cultural history:

In our passage two of the damned are introduced in the elevated style. Their earthly character is preserved in full force in their places in the beyond. Farinata is as great and proud as ever, and Cavalcante loves the light of the world and his son Guido not less, but in his despair still more passionately, than he did on earth. So God had willed; and so these things stand in the figural realism of Christian tradition. Yet never before has this realism been carried so far; never before—scarcely even in antiquity— has so much art and so much expressive power been employed to produce an almost painfully immediate impression of the earthly reality of human beings. It was precisely the Christian idea of the indestructibility of the entire human individual which made this possible for Dante. And it was precisely by producing this effect with such power and so much realism that he opened the way for that aspiration toward autonomy which possesses all earthly existence. In the very heart of the other world, he created a world of earthly beings and passions so powerful that it breaks bounds and proclaims its independence. . . . When we hear Cavalcante's outburst: *non fiere li occhi suoi il dolce lome*? or read the beautiful, gentle, and enchantingly feminine line which Pia de' Tolomei utters before she asks Dante to remember her on earth (*e riposato de la lunga via, Purg.*, 5, 131), we experience an emotion which is concerned with human beings and not directly with the divine order in which they have found their fulfillment. Their eternal position in the divine order is something of which we are only conscious as a setting whose irrevocability can but serve to heighten the effect of their humanity, preserved for us in all its force. The result is a direct experience of life which overwhelms everything else, a comprehension of human realities which spreads as widely and variously as it goes profoundly to the very roots of our emotions, an illumination of man's impulses and passions which leads us to share in them without restraint and indeed to admire their variety and their greatness.

And by virtue of this immediate and admiring sympathy with man, the principle, rooted in the divine order, of the indestructibility of the whole historical and individual man turns *against* that order, makes it subservient to its own purposes, and obscures it. The image of man eclipses the image of God. Dante's work made man's Christian-figural being a reality, and destroyed it in the very process of realizing it. The tremendous pattern was broken by the overwhelming power of the images it had to contain. The coarse disorderliness which resulted during the later Middle Ages from the farcical realism of the mystery plays is fraught with far less danger to the figural-Christian view of things than the elevated style of such a poet, in whose work men learn to see and know themselves. [*Mimesis,* pp. 199–202]

This kind of approach is still only in its beginnings, and I think it is worth pursuing. Its development as a powerful mode of historical appreciation will depend upon the extent to which we can find plausible bridges between literary style and meanings that have resonance as history. The problem is not unlike that faced by the New Criticism (by R. P. Warren, Cleanth Brooks, and William K. Wimsatt, Jr., for instance) in its attempt to find terms in which close literary analysis could be made correlative with judgments of the aesthetic, and then the moral value, of literary texts. Thus the usefulness of terms of impurity—"ambiguity," "paradox," "tension"—in the New Criticism, and their gradual equation with "maturity," which becomes thereby an evaluative as well as a descriptive term.

The stylistic problem is difficult in that style is itself difficult to grasp: no one has succeeded, so far as I know, in creating a master list of stylistic categories. There seems to be no limit to the ways in which style can exist in literature, and the ways in which it can be taken hold of. From essay to essay, depending on the tactical situation, Spitzer will find primary stylistic meaning in the temporal adverbs of a novel; the variety of proper nouns in another; three separate linguistic features of a classical play; the rhythmical pattern of an essay.[10] Similarly Auerbach in *Mimesis* uses variously tempo, dialect, logic, narrative stance, dramatic devices, and dozens of other traits in stylistic analysis. It may be that apart from the most obvious characteristics—syntactic habits, imagery, lexicon, and the like—stylistic categories are as much dependent on meaning as meaning is on style, and that stylistic criticism is a kind of dialectical strategy, in which the critic attends just as much to felt meanings while he tries to locate their stylistic bases as he attends to stylistic traits and wonders what meanings they may be helping to convey.

In either case the question is the same, what is the style saying and what does it mean? The possible areas of meaning themselves are correspondingly various. Some aspects of style may be functional only in the single work and be unique to it. Others seem characteristic of the whole *oeuvre* of an artist; they contribute to the style of the man. Others yet again may be point-

ing also to meanings beyond the work and the peculiar
situation of the individual artist and into the culture
itself. Thus, in something of a critical *tour de force,*
Auerbach in Chapter 3 of *Mimesis* can deduce from
the "gestural" diction and showy syntax, the "powerful
but distorted," "overrefined and exaggeratedly sensory"
style of a passage of Ammianus Marcellinus, the quality of hopeless, unredeemed defensiveness of Roman
civilization in the fourth century:

> Ammianus . . . belongs to the tradition of the
> antique historians in the elevated style, who look
> down from above and judge by moral standards,
> and who never make conscious and intentional use
> of the technique of realistic imitation because they
> scorn it as fit only for the low comic style. The par-
> ticular form of this tradition, which seems to have
> been especially favored in late Roman times (it is
> already embodied in Sallust, but especially in Taci-
> tus), is very strongly stoic in temper; it delights in
> choosing exceptionally somber subjects, which reveal
> a high degree of moral corruption, and then sharply
> contrasting them with its ideal concept of original
> simplicity, purity, and virtue. This is the pattern
> which Ammianus obviously wants to follow, as ap-
> pears from many passages of his work in which he
> cites deeds and sayings of earlier times in moralistic
> contrast. But from the very beginning we sense—
> and, in Ammianus, the impression becomes un-
> mistakable—that in this tradition the material
> increasingly masters the stylistic intent, until it
> finally overwhelms it and forces the style, with its
> pretension to reserve and refinement, to adapt itself
> to the content, so that diction and syntax, torn be-

tween the somber realism of the content and the
unrealistically refined tendency of the style, begin
to change and become inharmonious, overburdened,
and harsh. The diction grows mannered; the con-
structions begin, as it were, to writhe and twist. The
equable elegance is disturbed; the refined reserve
gives way to a somber pomp; and, against its will as
it were, the style renders a greater sensoriness than
would originally have been compatible with *gravitas,*
yet *gravitas* itself is by no means lost, but on the
contrary is heightened. The elevated style becomes
hyperpathetic and gruesome, becomes pictorial and
sensory. . . . Striking only in the sensory, resigned
and as it were paralyzed despite its stubborn rhetorical passion, his manner of writing history nowhere
displays anything redeeming, nowhere anything that
points to a better future, nowhere a figure or an act
about which stirs the refreshing atmosphere of a
greater freedom, a greater humanity. It had begun,
of course, in Tacitus, though by no means to the
same extent. And the cause of it is doubtless the
hopelessly defensive situation in which antique civilization found itself more and more deeply en-
meshed. No longer able to generate new hope and
new life from within, it had to restrict itself to measures which at best could only check decline and
preserve the status quo; but these measures too grow
more and more senile, their execution more and
more arduous . . . in Christianity itself—though
Ammianus would not seem to be unfriendly in his
attitude toward it—he sees nothing that might force
a way through the prevailing futureless darkness.
[pp. 56–57, 59–60]

This kind of connection between literary study and cultural history is my present subject; it is something of this sort that I shall be trying to explore in discussing in these essays three English poets—the *Pearl* poet, Langland, and Chaucer—in their setting in the late fourteenth century.

The age itself is apt for our inquiry, for two reasons. As ages go, it has pronounced character, for which we might expect to find clear stylistic symptoms; and it has pronounced resemblances to our own. It thus promises a special intensity of relevance. If not knowing history is to be condemned to relive it, then knowing this period may indeed save us some pains. I propose, then, to offer a brief characterization of the age—which I shall call an age of "crisis"—and then to investigate how each poet's style is related to it.

Of course, trying to characterize a whole age briefly is to deal in dangerous generalizations; as scholars and historians we do this unwillingly and at our peril. But every once in a while we must run the risk. Scholarly rigor and caution are admirable until they cut off contact between the researcher and his own culture. In any event, the general observations I shall offer herewith will be familiar ones. Though the study of specifically English culture in the late Middle Ages has for whatever reasons not yet produced a conspicuously broad, bold, and authoritative synthesis—an English cultural historian of Huizinga's breadth has yet to appear—there are numerous special studies, and some classical treatments of the enveloping continental culture of the period, on which to depend for guidance.

In calling Chaucer's age an age of "crisis" I may seem to be placing unwarranted confidence on a term that is more reliably used to describe people's reactions

to certain conditions than to describe the objective conditions themselves. There were surely people in that
age (as in our own) who lived through it without feeling that a crisis was going on. But for our purposes the
label will do to indicate on the one hand conditions
felt to be sufficient to generate a sense of crisis in the
people who went through them, and on the other hand
reliable testimony that a crisis was indeed felt.[11]

The age was one of contradiction as well as crisis,
and it was by no means an age simply of decline. We
would do well to recognize, for England in this period
and for the Western European community it belongs
to, some stabilizing events, and some signs of admirable accomplishment. The English parliament, particularly the House of Commons, is substantially the production of this period, as are some crucially important
techniques of organizing trade and finance. Philosophy
at Oxford and Paris, deriving in part from Ockhamite
thought of the earlier part of the century, continues
and enlarges the bases of modern scientific thought.
The century sees important developments in military
technique—with the introduction of the longbow and
the cannon—and in technology generally. This is the
century of the clock and the compass, of improved
navigation and shipping. For England it is the emergent age of the great cloth industry. In northern Europe pictorial art, architecture, and sculpture make
important gains in technique if not in spirituality. The
English language comes into its own as a literary and
administrative medium. The work of the very poets we
are discussing is a capital achievement of the culture;
apart from that of the fourteenth-century Tuscans, it is
not to be rivaled in the Middle Ages at all. In religion

the age sees the origin of movements that will issue in the Reformation.

Yet it persists in striking us more as an age of decline than of growth. It has a distinct character among periods of decline, in that decline does not come about gracefully. Rather, the elements of social and religious idealism are confronted with such great doses of intransigence, of nostalgia, of repression, or of bad luck as to create an atmosphere, not simply of decline, but of crisis. Thus the long economic depression that lasted from the end of the thirteenth till the middle of the fifteenth century was exacerbated by extraordinary attacks of famine in the first half of the fourteenth century and by the successive attacks of the Black Death, beginning in 1348–50, when perhaps a third of the population perished. The drastic speedup of the decline in population gave particular intensity to problems accompanying the slow but continuing decay of the feudal system. Agricultural workers in a period of labor shortage found their opportunities broadening, their expectations rising, their feudal obligations more irksome than ever. The response of the landlords and the government was repressive legislation. This is the century of the Jacquerie in France and of popular revolts all over Europe.[12]

In England in June of 1381 the peasants of Essex and Kent, goaded by antilabor laws, oppressive taxes, and other symptoms of corrupt and backward administration of the state, and led by radical reformers, revolted and marched on London. The government was taken completely by surprise. With the connivance of proletarian elements inside the city the mob came over the bridge and for two days were undisputed masters of a frightened city. Among the things they are reported to have demanded during the revolt were the handing over of all "traitors," the abolition of all lordships except the King's, the end of villeinage, the confiscation and distribution of Church property, and pardons for all. According to the chronicler Walsingham, the "mad" priest John Ball, one of the mob's leaders, preached before thousands at Blackheath a sermon from the text

> Whan Adam dalf, and Eve span,
> Wo was thanne a gentilman?

Ball thus converted an indigenous and hitherto rather harmless theme of Christian egalitarianism into a politically threatening call for social equality. "He tried," says Walsingham,

> to prove by the words of the proverb that he had taken for his text, that from the beginning all men were created equal by nature, and that servitude had been introduced by the unjust and evil oppression of men, against the will of God, who, if it had pleased Him to create serfs, surely in the beginning of the world would have appointed who should be a serf and who a lord. Let them consider, therefore, that He had now appointed the time wherein, laying aside the yoke of long servitude, they might, if they wished, enjoy their liberty so long desired. Wherefore they must be prudent, hastening to act after the manner of a good husbandman, tilling his field, and uprooting the tares that are accustomed to destroy the grain; first killing the great lords of the realm, then slaying the lawyers, justices and jurors, and finally rooting out everyone whom they knew to be harmful to the community in future. So at last they would

obtain peace and security, if, when the great ones
had been removed, they maintained among themselves equality of liberty and nobility, as well as of
dignity and power.

And when he had preached these and many other
ravings, he was in such high favour with the common
people that they cried out that he should be archbishop and Chancellor of the kingdom, and that he
alone was worthy of the office, for the present archbishop was a traitor to the realm and the commons,
and should be beheaded wherever he could be
found.[13]

Whether or not under Ball's influence, the mob settled scores with the most prominent of their oppressors:
they burned the palace of the Duke of Lancaster John
of Gaunt, the greatest magnate of the realm and the
patron of Chaucer, and beheaded, among many others,
Chancellor Sudbury, Archbishop of Canterbury, as he
took refuge in the tower with the royal family and
council. Meanwhile the fourteen-year-old King Richard was negotiating with the rebel leaders. Aided by
the rebels' touching confidence that the crown would
put all to rights, Richard watched his men kill the
principal rebel leader on the very next day. Proclaim-
ing himself their chief, he granted all their demands,
supplied them with charters, and sent them trium-
phantly home. The wave of revolt, killing, and burning
that had spread to other parts of the country soon
stopped. Then came the government's turn: the pardons were revoked, the judges set to work, and the
movement's leaders were tried and executed. Walsingham reports that when a group from Essex asked
whether the King intended to honor his charters,

Richard answered: "Rustics you were and rustics you are still."[14]

"[The revolt] came as the last of three successive indictments of the government within a decade," writes May McKisack in her Oxford History volume, ". . . it created an atmosphere of general nervousness which long outlasted its suppression."[15] It thus serves to document the political as well as the economic crisis of the age. The century had seen Edward II deposed and murdered, and Edward III pursuing into his dotage an endless and ruinous war with the French. The latter part of Richard II's reign would see the French war relatively in abeyance, but the perennial struggle among nobles and crown continued in aggravated form in the appellants' successful revolt in 1387, in the merciless Parliament that followed, in Richard's subsequent recovery and revenge, and in the revolution which saw him finally deposed and executed.

In almost painful contrast to the corrupt and incompetent administration of government, and the prevalent cynicism and brutality of politics in the period, there is a surge of romantic and nostalgic cultivation of the outward forms of chivalry. This is the age of sumptuous tournaments, of the Order of the Garter, and the King's heralds, of the Court of Chivalry (before which Chaucer testified in a coat-of-arms dispute), and the sale of patents of nobility. Such pronounced concern with social status and its outward badges may well be a symptom of insecurity in a class massively beset by unrest from below. In any case the ethical norms of the cult of chivalry point up the disparity between the period's ideals and its actions. As Gervase Mathew charitably observes, "It was perhaps a central tension in late fourteenth-century English culture that its economics, its politics and its fiction were all too complex for so simple and individualistic a code."[16]

The condition of the fourteenth-century Church is too well known to need elaborate emphasis. The century begins with the captivity of the papacy at Avignon and ends with the Great Schism, in which Europe was treated to the spectacle of two popes excommunicating and making war on each other. The virtual destruction of the papacy as a spiritual force is only the symptom, however, of general decline in ecclesiastical prestige. There were of course great prelates and great priests in England. But their presence serves mostly to underline the Church's defects, from the secular and political pursuits of the episcopate to the widespread poverty of parish priests and the neglect of the parishes themselves.

The desperate case of the priests is exemplified in the Peasants' Revolt. It was a priest, John Wrawe, who led the mob which sacked the rich monastery of Bury St. Edmunds and beheaded its prior. John Ball, reports Walsingham, preached that "tithes ought not to be paid to an incumbent unless he who should give them were richer than the rector or vicar who received them; and that tithes and offerings ought to be withheld if the parishioner were known to be a man of better life than his priest. . . ."[17] Every reader of the literature of the period knows its satire on corrupt clerics: friars, pardoners, summoners, absentee priests. The period is full of complaint against pluralism, nonresidence, the sale of benefices, the baronial scale of monastic possessions, and ecclesiastical wealth. Anticlericalism there had always been, but in this period it is deepened by the growth of a theological and political rationale, and by the intransigence with which demands for reform were met and suppressed. In the eleventh century the highest officials of the Church had headed the reform movement; now the official position is everywhere one of reaction. Heterodoxy there had always been, but now because of the growing incapacity of the orthodox element to practice what it preaches, and because of the Church's failure to find a place or an outlet for reformist enthusiasm, it is being driven into heretical movements that finally issue into the Reformation.[18]

The Oxford professor John Wyclif is the great English reformist writer of the period. From 1374 on, he moves from an anticlericalism which earned him papal censure to denial of the doctrine of transubstantiation, and, just at the moment of the Peasants' Revolt, to the open heresy of his *Confessio*. He escaped trial as a heretic only through the influence of powerful friends like John of Gaunt, and, forbidden to preach or teach, spent his remaining three years of life in a tireless production of further documentary proofs of his fierce dissent. Himself no practical reformer nor leader of men, his obdurate teachings—that the Roman Church was capable of errors in articles of faith, that the Bible (which he caused first to be translated into English) was more authoritative than bishop, council or Pope —provided the nucleus for the heretical Lollard movement, which, despite its decline through assiduous persecution by Church and state, nevertheless survived into the English Reformation.[19]

The emergence of Lollardy in England was typical of many similar manifestations of the period in its basic ideas and values and its steady progression into open heresy. Not only institutional defects of the Church, but indeed the thought and spiritual temper of the time drove men to a crisis of faith. Heterodox ideas, some deriving from the Ockhamite, Joachite, and Spiritual-Franciscan thought of earlier periods, flourished and compounded themselves in an atmosphere of dependence on inner rather than on ecclesiastical authority. The cleavage between reason and faith, characteristic of post-Ockhamite thought, not only generated a certain unsettling scepticism, but also drove faith itself further and further into the realm of the irrational.Thus the age is one of the resurgence of a mysticism which, as Gordon Leff puts it, "was subjective, often to the point of being indistinguishable from histrionics."[20] The histrionic tone of late-medieval religiosity is fed in turn by a new resurgence of apocalypticism which the Black Death did much to validate.

In looking at the religious iconography and the art of the period, we shall have to stand back from late-fourteenth-century England, and take in materials from continental sources and from the surrounding periods. Because of the infrequent survival of substantial native works of art, and because in many ways the period is one of the free admission of continental artists and styles, it is difficult to characterize the native English painting and sculpture with any security. My general impression of the art of Richard II's reign is that it shows mainly the conservative side of the mood of the time; it does not much suggest a milieu of turbulence or crisis. Similarly English architecture, now in its great "early Perpendicular" period, suggests solidity and dignity rather than tension or decay.[21] Nevertheless the English, with French and Netherlandish, is part of a northern Gothic art which is entering its "late" phase, and it is in this loose but still meaningful sense that we can summarize the artistic manifestations of the culture of the age.

In the religious iconography of the time, as in religious thought, we find a shifting toward the emotional —Emile Mâle describes it in terms of an exaggerated Franciscanism—the emotional and finally the macabre. "The serene art of the thirteenth century," says Mâle, "is followed by the impassioned, unhappy art (*l'art passioné, douloureux*) of the fourteenth and fifteenth."[22] The progression of tone and style in medieval art in the fourteenth century is not a regular one and not easy to follow in its details, but the general direction is unmistakable. Comparing the religious art of the thirteenth century to that of the fifteenth, says Mâle, "one is almost tempted to ask whether it is the same religion that the artists are interpreting." The art of the thirteenth century rarely represents pain and death, and when it does, they are sublimated, dominated by a serene confidence. Even the Passion of Jesus itself fails to awaken painful feelings, he remarks. "In the fifteenth century," he continues,

> the majority of extant works are somber and tragic; art offers us no more than the image of pain and death. Jesus no longer teaches; he suffers: or rather, he seems to be setting before us his wounds and his blood as the supreme teaching. What we are going to come upon from now on is Jesus naked, bleeding, crowned with thorns, the instruments of his Passion, and his corpse laid out in his mother's lap. . . . The high middle ages represented almost nothing but Christ triumphant, the thirteenth century found its master work in the type of Christ teaching, the

fifteenth century wished to see in its God only the man of suffering. From now on Christianity is presented in its pathetic aspect.[23]

Mâle cites further evidence in the late-fourteenth-century emergence of the Passion of the Virgin Mary or the *pietà,* first in painting, then in sculpture—a motif especially congenial to the mystics. The Pietà often displays along with suffering and death the new tenderness and familiarity, the new softness and sentimentality, that is clearly to be found in the representation of the Virgin and child, and of the saints.[24] At the same time pictorial art, pointing toward the superbly realistic painting of Jean Fouquet and Jan Van Eyck, is becoming an art of extremes, of the dissolution of high Gothic poise. The northern realism of the fifteenth century is a realism that finally denies the piety of its subject matter, or is rather the expression of a piety "so direct that no earthly figure is too sensual or too heavy to express it."[25] Sculpture too, freeing itself from architecture, is becoming increasingly realistic, but it is a realism with less and less spirituality. Gothic architecture on the Continent, finally, is dissolving into the tracery of the flamboyant style.

The literature of the age matches its art, particularly in the later stages. Chaucer's French contemporaries, Deschamps, Machaut, and Froissart—his first models —show some technical liveliness, but they are still largely dominated by the courtly forms and attitudes of a century before. They write a charming poetry (and Froissart a prose) that must be counted among the symptoms of the period's conservatism which we have already noticed. The same is true of John Gower, Chaucer's friend and the most important English poet after the ones that particularly concern us. Deschamps, who knew Chaucer's poems, does at the same time have a distinct bent for satire and complaint, but it too seems conventional, and does not link up with the age's deeper currents of social unrest. It provides a bridge, however, to the literature of the following age —the age of Villon, let us say—which shows clearly the inharmonious exaggerations of motifs that in the high Gothic period had been held in balance. As has often been observed, it is on the one hand a literature of complicated verse-forms, extravagant rhetoric, endless romances and decorative allegories of love. At the same time it is a literature of thickening realism, of crude satire, of deepening grossness, obscenity, scatology. Its humor is more trivial or more macabre, sometimes bordering on the pathological and sadistic. Its seriousness is one of melancholic disenchantment, of preoccupation with old age, decay, and death. It was about 1400, according to Huizinga, that pictorial art achieved a realism grisly enough to render realistically the details of human decomposition; at about the same time the motif spread from ecclesiastical to secular literature. The *danse macabre* was first so named in a French poem of 1376.[26] From all we can guess, all three of our poets, the greatest that medieval England produced, were living and writing at this moment.

If, as I have tried to show, the age has a pronounced character, so do the *Pearl* poet, Langland, and Chaucer. Our question is in what ways are they to be understood as poets of that time and that place? How do their works fit into a full and complex sense of their time? From the point of view of our methodological concern as students of literature: how has what we otherwise know of the culture left evidence of its condition in their art, and particularly in their style? And how does their art, reciprocally, modify and enrich our notion of their culture?

Our answers will be complicated, to say the least, by the difficulty, inherent in all studies of style-and-culture, of allowing for the particular character and situation of the individual artist. Although medieval decorum discouraged artistic idiosyncrasy, we can sense at once radical differences in the personalities of these three. There are also radical differences in the amount we actually know about them personally, and in the degree and kind of report of contemporary life found in their works. Each of them is in various ways still quite mysterious, for each in his own medieval way eschews journalism for an art more general and exemplary. All three are exasperatingly bare of direct allusions to specific contemporary people and events.

In the area of direct relationship to the history of the age we should expect most of Chaucer, who is incomparably the best known and most prolific of the three. We have a splendid new edition of the official records of his life.[27] While it is true that not a single one of these six hundred pages contains reference to his having been a poet, we have an excellent picture of his career as courtier and public servant. He came from a prominent commercial family with some connections at court. We first find him, in 1357, a page in the household of the countess of Ulster. He served in the army in France; was captured and ransomed; passed into the service of Edward III, making a series of trips to the Continent on diplomatic missions. For many years he was close to the family of John of Gaunt; his wife's sister, Katharine Swynford, was successively mistress and third wife of that important nobleman.

Chaucer's knowledge of court and of international politics must have been equalled by his knowledge of commerce and of public works. In middle and late life he held a variety of responsible posts: Controller of Customs and Subsidy of Wools, Skins, and Hides in the port of London; Controller of the Petty Custom on Wines; Clerk of the King's Works; Deputy Forester of the royal forest of North Petherton. He was for four years a justice of the peace for Kent, and he sat in Parliament for Kent in the session of 1386. Shortly thereafter, he seems to have suffered financial reverses. But he survived extremely well the violent political vicissitudes of the reign of Richard II, including the deposing of Richard. In 1399, a year before Chaucer's death, the new king, Henry IV, renewed and increased his annuity from the crown.

Chaucer's earliest substantial poem, the vaguely allegorical *Book of the Duchess,* only thinly veils its occasion: it is an elegy on the death in 1369 of Blanche, Duchess of Lancaster, wife of John of Gaunt. It must have been composed within the year following. Similarly, "occasional" origin has been suggested for his unfinished *House of Fame,* which appears to be leading up to some momentous political or social announcement; and his *Parliament of Fowls* is a St. Valentine's Day poem, we do not know for what year. Actual prototypes have been suggested for some of his characters. But it is a good index of the paucity of contemporary reference in Chaucer that despite some of the most elegant scholarly research of our time, we cannot establish the precise date of the composition of a single one of his substantial poems.[28] The momentous crises and catastrophes of his time scarcely peep out of these pages; his only undoubted reference to the Peasant's Revolt is in a simile in the *Nun's Priest's Tale* describing the noise of the country folk in pursuit of Reynard the Fox:

> Certes, he Jakke Strawe and his meynee
> Ne made nevere shoutes half so shrille
> Whan that they wolden any Flemyng kille,
> As thilke day was maad upon the fox.
>
> [3394–3397]

The reference is to the massacre of Flemish dockworkers by the London mob, a shameful little side-event in the occupation of the city. Here it seems naked of political or social significance, as if Chaucer were almost unaware of such.

Chaucer makes charming reference, occasionally, to his own life. He can be glimpsed at work over his accounts in the customhouse; he characterizes himself as a great reader; he makes fun of his fatness and his unlikeliness as a lover. One of the most interesting accomplishments of Chaucer critics in recent years is the uncovering and the delineation of the "Chaucer" to be found in Chaucer's works. But it is becoming ever more clear that this Chaucer is not the historical fourteenth-century courtier and man of letters but an artifact. This artifact, this fictional character or *persona,* is almost as much a creation of Chaucer the artist as are Pandarus and the Wife of Bath. He is, in fact, a major implement of Chaucer's narrative technique. There is no doubt that Chaucer, who must have recited some of these poems to friends, continually employs and manipulates traits of the historical Chaucer—i.e., of himself—in a genial interplay between reciter and audience. But just as Chaucer the Canterbury pilgrim is exposed as a hopelessly bad poet, so we cannot be certain that any of the traits of the historical Chaucer are being given to us "straight."

We can be more certain, indeed, that the artifact Chaucer differs fundamentally from his historical namesake. The shy, bumbling bookworm of the early poems, the naive, transparently deferential, bourgeois good fellow of the *Canterbury Tales* could never have survived in Chaucer's actual milieu. As Kittredge memorably put it, "a naif Collector of Customs would be a paradoxical monster."[29] But I am not convinced that the portrait that Professor Talbot Donaldson sensi‑ tively deduces from an awareness of the fiction itself is as realistic a reconstruction as we might make. The Chaucer his audience knew, says Donaldson, was

> a bourgeois, but one who was known as a practical and successful man of the court; possessed perhaps of a certain diffidence of manner, reserved, deferen‑ tial to the socially imposing persons with whom he was associated; a bit absent-minded, but affable and, one supposes, very good company—a good fellow; sagacious and highly perceptive.[30]

This is probably true as far as it goes. But loving Chaucer as we truly do, we have not yet asked all the questions. If a naif customs official would be a para‑ doxical monster, one muses, a blameless one in this period would be—at the very least—surprising. Leaf‑ ing through the *Life Records* one comes on the ques‑ tion of why Chaucer was not reelected to Parliament after the session of 1386. There were accusations made before that very Parliament of widespread corruption in the customs offices. Was it merely because of his identification with the King's party, or because of his conduct of office, that he shortly thereafter gave up his controllerships of customs? Why was Chaucer awarded in 1376 such a handsome reward as £71.4.6, the entire proceeds of the conviction of John Kent of London for exporting wool without paying customs duties? What elements in our portrait of Chaucer the man take into account his part (whatever it was) in the rape (or perhaps abduction) of Cecily Chaumpaigne?[31]

These are all small matters in the light of the kind of history we are pursuing, and I am not about to pursue them. In the absence of documentary evidence, biographical speculation is perhaps amusing, but not profitable. However, that no one has felt prepared to take an unbiased look at the personal trivia simply underlines the fact that we do not know the man in terms of many of his major, concrete activities. We do not know whether he was courageous or cowardly, and to what extent he practiced that Christian charity ultimately recommended in many of his works. We do not know how deeply he was implicated in the major social and religious issues of the time. We do not know what he thought of Wyclif, who was long protected for political reasons by John of Gaunt. (Chaucer was for a time a close associate of some Lollard knights; but on the other hand the Host in the *Canterbury Tales* makes fun of Lollardy.) One returns to the fact that we do not know where he was during the Peasants' Revolt, nor what he may have thought of or learnt from it. Is Chaucer in any other sense a poet of an age of crisis? How deeply is he relevant to his time?

That Chaucer *is* a man of his time has been proved repeatedly in the archaeological sense. Of course we praise the artist for his transcendance of journalism;

for his capacity for symbolism—his capacity to invest the concrete image with broader meaning; his gift for giving what successive generations have felt to be insight into general human nature in his portraits of fourteenth-century characters. Yet at the same time we feel his picture of the times in general—its manners, morals, customs, speech—to be tellingly accurate. He is part of the time a master realist and comic satirist, and what we know from other sources corroborates his report: prioresses, monks, innkeepers, and even pardoners did indeed behave that way then.

This validation of the historical truth of Chaucer in his genre-painting is supported by another kind of validation to be deduced from the ideas and doctrines found scattered in his works. Chaucer was not a philosopher, but he was a great reader, a great considerer of ideas, and his ideas are safely and authentically medieval. Almost no one calls him a harbinger of the Renaissance any more. His fundamental position is Christian and a bit stoical. Trying to summarize his ideology, one might conclude that it was almost too safely a medieval, conservative one, perhaps more in tune with an earlier and securer phase of medieval culture. The only suggestion of its approaching the thinking of an age of crisis is its profound dependence on and affinity for the sixth-century *Consolation of Philosophy* of Boethius—itself supremely a product of cultural crisis, in which the last great thinker of the antique world, a Roman senator imprisoned by an Ostrogothic king, facing almost certain death on charges of treason, summons up all his philosophy in an effort to reconcile himself to God's ways. The book has been a comfort to men in every age since, yet the depth of Chaucer's sympathy with it, the pervasiveness of its influence on him, would, if we had no other evidence, argue in Chaucer some sense of the insecurity, the contradictoriness, and the brittleness of his own situation.

It is this sense which makes Chaucer seem most deeply sensitive to history, and we feel it in him at every turn. It is there pervasively and massively, not so much in his rather genial and tolerant realism, suggested only by inference and by turns in his Boethian conclusions and in the thematic material of some of his poems, but expressed in large and small in the texture of his poetry and in its gross structure by what I shall call here, summarizing, his ironic style. This style at its best embraces, inspects, and holds out for our delectation a world of alternate possibilities. It compares and tests the major value systems then in conflict —the Christian, the secular-idealist, and the secular-materialist—and does so with such comprehensiveness, clarity, and sympathy, that we must be satisfied that he, like the Wife of Bath, has had his world in his time. His poised, conservative, orthodox Boethian conclusions are validated by his confrontation of the major issues of value, and this confrontation is conveyed by Chaucer the artist in the style and structure, the typically ironic composition, of such masterpieces as the *Troilus* and the *Canterbury Tales*.

Chaucer the supreme ironist is of course not new to us. I have made my own argument for the dominant irony of his style elsewhere,[32] and will not repeat more of it here. What I shall offer instead, in a later chapter, are some reflections deriving from the fact that Chaucer was not always successful at irony, nor always an ironist. What alternatives did he try, I shall ask, and what further meanings may they suggest as to his relation to late medieval culture?

If the abundant documentary records of Chaucer, and his celebrated realism, yield so little direct evidence of his response to the age, we might well be discouraged at the case of our other two poets, for here there are, besides the manuscripts of the poems, no documents at all. We are not certain of the name of the author of *Piers Plowman,* if there was only one author, and if the work is one work rather than being two or three or four. At one time I felt, without regard to the so-called internal and external evidence, that no man in his right mind would twice *re*write a long, doctrinal poem—producing three versions in the course of twenty years, versions moreover which have defied all our efforts to find a consistent principle, either artistic or doctrinal or even political, governing the revision. Wordsworth produced less revision of the *Prelude* in fifty years, and that poem had not already been published to the world. Surely, among medieval texts the three versions of *Piers Plowman,* if written by one man, must be unique in this respect. Studying the poem a little more, however, one finds it to be unique in so many respects that one begins rather to feel that if anyone in the middle ages would have written and twice rewritten a long doctrinal poem it could only have been the author of *Piers Plowman.* Such evidence as there is, recently summarized by Professor Kane,[33] supports the idea of single authorship; I am content to call the shadowy historical figure who thus emerges by the name of William Langland, the more so because he seems so palpably in his poem to have placed before us directly his own personality and his own ideas.

We know Langland the man in ways that we do not know Chaucer. He is a moralist, a sermoner, a satirist, and a reformer, and there is little in his culture that we do not have his firsthand opinion about. Our investigation of Langland in terms of the literature of an age of crisis would seem to be almost redundant. On every leaf he deals with contemporary moral, political, and religious problems, which he envisions as parts of a single indictment of his age. We shall not need to dwell on this aspect of a poem that is mined for evidence by the social and cultural historians themselves. We shall, rather, turn from Langland the reformer to Langland the artist, and ask how they agree—to ask what (if anything) the poem as artifact has to add obliquely or stylistically to what the poem as moral tract directly says.

Speaking of poems as artifacts leads us naturally to our third poet, the author of *Pearl, Sir Gawain and the Green Knight,* and of a few lesser didactic poems: *Purity, Patience*, and perhaps *St. Erkenwald.* Of him we know precisely nothing, nor would we have any of his poems were it not for the unique manuscript of them that survived the great fire in the Cotton Collection in 1731. The poems, written in archaic or revivalist English verse-forms, and in a difficult provincial dialect, the dialect of the West Midlands, were not printed until the nineteenth century and have only recently—in the last twenty-five years—been properly appreciated as works of art.

Pearl and *Sir Gawain* are in a sense discoveries of the New Criticism; under close analysis they have been shown to have a depth and sophistication rivaling that of the best poems of Chaucer. Their author, like Langland, may conceivably have been a cleric. He is an orthodox Christian and knows both English and continental literary tradition. At the same time he has close affinities with feudal, aristocratic pursuits. He understands hunting and courtly love and country life. To judge by the contents of his poems, he may have been a priest attached to some back-country baronial court, far from the centers of power and the play of contemporary history. Entirely unlike Langland's, his poetry appears to say almost nothing of the late fourteenth century. It includes an Arthurian romance, a moral-allegorical vision-poem on personal salvation, and religious exempla based on Scripture and hagiology. The *Gawain* castle is thought architecturally to be a late-medieval one, but this and other touches of contemporary texture in the poetry are trivial.

Pearl and *Sir Gawain* present in perhaps the most acute form the problem of the relevance of poetry to cultural history; they seem so completely poetry, works of art, and so little history. Do they speak in any way to the actual condition of the age of Chaucer? This is the question to which we shall turn in the next chapter.

II

THE *PEARL* POET: STYLE AS DEFENSE

THE MORALIST AND THE ARTIST IN THE PEARL POET are so intimately related—the art of the poems and their meaning are so much entwined—that there is a certain violence in trying to part them. I shall do so only temporarily, considering briefly the moralist alone in order to show finally how much his true position depends on that of the artist.

The *Pearl* moralist, then, seems from his overt statements to be a surprisingly uncomplicated moralist, and a conservative one as well. Thinking of his having lived in the second half of the fourteenth century, we find him surprisingly untroubled for those troubled times, and surprisingly accepting and unquestioning of the orthodox forms of Christianity and of feudalism. These two major systems of thought, feeling, belief, and behavior were undergoing such trials and such patent damage in his time that his relatively slight reflection of actual conditions would seem to argue a kind of escapism or reaction.

It could not have been simple ignorance. A provincial court of sufficient culture to have evoked these poems is not likely to have been unaware of plague, corruption, war, revolt, schism. Indeed, if we look beyond the two masterpieces to the two lesser poems, we find ample reference to disaster and to moral decay. We may be hearing an indictment of the militarism of his own times in the poet's description in *Purity* of the brutality of Adam's descendants before the Flood:

He watz famed for fre þat feȝt loved best,
And ay þe bigest in bale þe best watz halden.

[275–276][1]

[He who best loved fighting got a reputation for nobility; and ever the greatest doer of harm was considered the best man.]

Perhaps in his moving accounts of the dark anger of God—in his descriptions of the welter of the Flood, of the destruction of Sodom and Gomorrah and of the reigns of Zedekiah and Belshazzar, of the storm in *Patience* and the stink of the whale—we sense his own passionate concern with crimes and punishments of his contemporaries.[2]

But even when he is cataloguing specific vices to be avoided, in the manner of a preacher, his thrust is so general that we can make nothing distinctively local or contemporary out of it:

For fele fautez may a freke forfete his blysse,
Þat he þe Soverayn ne se—þen for slauþe one,
As for bobaunce and bost, and bolnande pryde,
Þroly into þe develez þrote man þryngez bylyve;
For covetyse, and colwarde and croked dedez,
For mon-sworne, and men-sclaȝt, and to much drynk,
For þefte, and for þrepyng, unþonk may mon have;
For roborrye, and riboudrye, and resounez untrwe,
And dysheriete and depryve dowrie of wydoez,
For marryng of maryagez, and mayntnaunce of
        schrewez,
For traysoun and trichcherye, and tyrauntyre boþe,
And for fals famacions and fayned lawez—
Man may mysse þe myrþe þat much is to prayse
For such unþewez as þise, and þole much payne,

And in þe Creatores cort com never more,
Ne never see hym with syȝt for such sour tornez.
                                        [*Purity*, 177–192]

> [For many faults a man may forfeit Paradise so that he
> see not the Sovereign: one is sloth; for presumption and
> boasting, and swollen pride, man swiftly rushes direct
> into the devil's throat; a man may come to harm for
> covetousness, and villainy, and crooked deeds, for per-
> jury, and manslaughter, and too much drink, for theft,
> and for quarreling; for robbery, and lechery, and false-
> hood, and despoiling and depriving widows of their
> doweries, for ruining marriages and supporting wicked
> people, for treason and treachery, and tyranny as well,
> and for false laws—for such vices as these men may miss
> the joy that is greatly to be valued, and suffer much
> pain, and nevermore come into the court of the Creator,
> nor, for such vile deeds, never set eyes on him.]

His poems are completely devoid of identifiable personal or political references. Ten verses near the opening of *Purity* (vv. 7–16) contain his only allusion to
the vices of the clergy.[3]

On balance, furthermore, in his treatment of virtue
and vice he addresses himself to the personal crisis
more readily than to the social. Where in *Piers Plowman* we are continually reminded of the ordained function, behavior, and failure of groups, estates, profes-
sions—the *Pearl* poet's imagination polarizes around
the moral condition of the individual: Jonah, the
Pearl-Dreamer, Sir Gawain. He has a feeling for lone-
liness. Even in the most "social" of the poems, *Purity,*
the argument periodically centers on single protago-
nists. Of course all of the individuals in this poetry are
highly exemplary, but for the most part they exemplify
crises of the private human will and judgment. While

any of these *could* be generalized into social maladies, the poet does not in fact present himself as a satirist, a reformer, or even as a complainer of the badness of the times. In the two masterpieces that principally concern us, there is very little preaching on deadly sins and very little sense of retribution. Moralist he remains to the core, but somehow detached from current history.

His religious ideas, particularly on free grace, which were once thought to border on heresy—Carleton Brown called him an evangelist and anticipator of Protestantism—have now been found to be safely orthodox.[4] There is perhaps a flavor of protestantism in that his overt theology is not much a matter of the Church, the Fathers, and the Doctors, but rather depends much on Scripture. The moral fervor of *Pearl,* and the depth of its symbolism, would plausibly relate it to the flowering of devotional literature in the fourteenth century. But in it he never reaches that degree of mysticism or emotionalism, never really suggests that excess of feeling that we have come to associate with late-medieval religiosity.[5] He does not linger at all over Death's decay of the flesh; the Passion, briefly regarded along with the bleeding wound of the Lamb (vv. 805–814, 1135–1137), is not touched with horror or grotesqueness. Even the pathos that we should normally expect in an elegy, though unmistakably and movingly present, is restrained, muted in ways that we shall notice when we turn to the art of the poem.

I need not insist on the *Pearl* poet's allegiance to high-medieval feudalism. It is to be discovered just under the surface in *Pearl,* implicit in the diction and in the relationship of the characters. God and the elect are themselves conceived as a feudal hierarchy, which has taken to itself, spiritualized, and perfected that ideal of Courtesy[6] which it now shares with high-medieval aristocracy. The same fusion of religious with feudal idealism is even more apparent in *Sir Gawain*. We might be tempted to see in the poet of this highly heraldic poem, with its emblematic band worn cross-wise, its color green, its pentangular symbol, some of the gaudy ceremoniality of the period; but if so, the moralist has raised the ceremony to something finer than the typically late-medieval assertion of rank and ·class-consciousness.

The *Pearl* poet as moralist is a remarkably pure and uncompromising moralist. He seems in fact to have a passion for purity. It is, in a way, all he ever writes about: in *Patience* it is the purity of Jonah's obedience to the Lord; in *Cleanness* (or *Purity*), the impurity and the corrective cleansing of God's vassals; in *Pearl,* the salvation of the pure, and in *Sir Gawain,* the slight impurity of Gawain's *trawþe*. In the latter two poems —which turn on delicate distinctions, degrees of purity —we find much of the obverse and concomitant motif, of spottedness and imperfection. Whatever critics decide to be the precise sin of Gawain—be it pride, cowardice, carnal frailty, or what not—he wears the green girdle "In tokenyng he watz tane in tech of a faute" (v. 2488). The innocents in *Pearl* are "Wythouten note oþer mascle of sulpande synne" (v. 727). The pearl in its various manifestations is *wythouten spot, maskeles, wemles, unblemyst*; it has no *teche* or stain. This imagery of spotlessness is dominant enough to constitute the refrain linking the stanzas in three sections of the poem, including the very first, and it is a strong factor in the contrast of the two main groups of images; in Wendell Stacy Johnson's terms:

on the one hand, images out of the world of growing
things, images of the garden and the vineyard which
are associated with the dust of the earth; on the
other, images of light and of brilliant, light-reflecting
gems, free of any spot (dust) and associated with
whiteness and with emblems of royalty.[7]

There is no question, in any of his poems, of his fundamental purism. In morals, tolerant of human imperfection as he may be, he is always aware of the ideal:
the pure, the perfect.

It is not surprising that these terms can be applied
to him wholly as artist as well. His awareness of integrity in morals seems to be of a piece, in his total personality, with his sense of form. He is almost unique
among medieval poets in having a passion for unity,
for utter discipline of form. I say "almost unique"
thinking of Dante, of Dante's moral purism, of the formal regularity of the *Commedia*, which is emblematic
of the rightness of the universe, and of the stunning
interplay of formal correspondences within this regularity which amplify and celebrate unity, order, the
regular correspondences of all things. Even in verse-
form the two poets have comparable impulses. Dante's
extraordinary feat in never repeating a rime (the endless fecundity of God's sounds!) and the endless linkage of the *terza rima* have something of the same effect
as the extraordinary linkedness of lines and stanzas
in *Pearl*.

Both *Pearl* and *Gawain* end on a note reminiscent
of their beginnings. They come full circle like Gawain's
pentangle, an endless knot, and remind us of the round-
ness and integrity of themselves. Within this integrity, the poet has furthermore, in each case, set himself

difficult formal tasks, the performance of which is a kind of celebration, as in Dante, of the ultimate unity of the work—whether it be God's or the poet's. In *Pearl* much of this performance is in the verse-form itself. Each twelve-line stanza has only three rimes, one of them used no less than six times per stanza. The stanzas are grouped by fives, the last line of each stanza in the group being connected to the first line of the next by a repeated syllable, word, or phrase, and all the stanzas in the group ending with a repeated phrase, something like a refrain. Since the last riming syllables in the stanzas are always part of this repeated phrase, all the stanzas in a group are further linked by having the same rime in lines 10 and 12. There are twenty of these groups, which are themselves linked at beginning and end by similarly repeated phrases. This metrical form is "probably the most complex in English."[8] The metrical task in *Sir Gawain* involves stanzas of unrimed alliterative long-lines followed by a brief rimed "bob and wheel," scarcely less complicated than in *Pearl*. In *Sir Gawain* the echoing alliteration, the linking of words by sound, has much of the same repetitive, unifying effect as have the rimes and refrains in *Pearl*.

The sense of order, correspondence, and linkage in both poems is powerfully supported by a certain amount of numerical symbolism. It would not be surprising to find such symbolism in the work of a poet who could give us the description of the pentangle, Sir Gawain's device, along with the exegesis (vv. 619–665) explaining that it stands for five interlocking sets of five interlocking virtues. But the poet's interest in repeated pattern goes well beyond mystical numbers to produce those repetitions of words, images, scenes, and actions that every reader recognizes and that seem to constitute a dominant artistic habit. In *Pearl* there is the astonishing ubiquity of the pearl symbol itself, and the pattern of successive gardens which are the locus of the action. In *Sir Gawain* patterns of time, place, and action are everywhere: "Things are arranged in pairs—there are two New Year's days, two beheading scenes, two courts, two confessions; or in threes—three temptations, three hunts, three kisses, three strokes of the ax."[9] There is a major sequence of repeated actions in the arming of Gawain and description of his shield, his journey to the castle, his three temptations, and his confession to the priest—taken up again in his second arming and the description of the girdle, his journey to the Green Chapel, the three strokes of the ax, and his confession to the Green Knight. There is continued patterning in the exchange of gifts in the castle, the exchange of visits between Gawain and the challenger, and so on and on.

To pursue this theme longer would be to defer unduly the observation that, despite this extraordinary insistence on unity, pattern, order, regularity, the poetry in its full effect has nothing of the monotony, the stiffness, the rigidity or intransigence or dogmatism that we might expect such a formal structure to support. Trying to account for this will bring us closer to the center of the poet's art and meaning.

The poet's use of some important elementary contrasts may contribute to his avoidance of a monochromatic effect; surely it contributes to his avoidance of simplicity and monotony. We have already mentioned the elementary contrast of nature and super-nature, heaven and earth, in the imagery of *Pearl*. *Sir Gawain* is similarly planned across contrasts between civilization and wildness, warmth and cold, company and solitude. But these and other contrasts have so powerful an effect that they may at the same time be taken as reinforcing rather than blurring the sense of pattern in the poem. Earth and heaven, spottedness and purity, the old hag and the beautiful hostess, winter storm and Christmas fireside juxtaposed in this poetry, as often intensify as modify each other. This leads me to feel that it is not only the elementary contrasts in the patterns of the poetry, but also the almost incredible richness of oblique *variation* on these patterns that accounts for the poetry's final effect: not of a simplistic black and white purism, but of a purism that comprehends the whole shimmering range of possibilities in the variants from pattern or perfection. Thinking now of the total effect of these poems and how unobtrusive the patterning often is, we might guess that it exists as much to provide a basis for the variation as vice versa. My thesis here, at any rate, is that the interplay between formal unity and variation is at the core of both the style and the meaning of the poetry,[10] and I shall point to some characteristics in *Pearl* and *Sir Gawain* in turn to illustrate.

" 'O spotless pearl in flawless pearls, that wears,' said I, 'the precious pearl' "—

> 'O maskeleȝ perle in perleȝ pure,
> Þat bereȝ,' quod I, 'þe perle of prys.'
>
> [745–746]

The poet who could write those lines and get away with it—nay, set them vibrating with meanings as subtly related to each other as are their sound-effects— is a poet for whom variation is a passion, and whose

feeling for language is marked by the same play of repetition, synonymy, and symbolic variation that we find
in the grosser pattern of the poetry. The extraordinary
rhymes and refrains (and, as here, the occasional alliteration) of the *Pearl* verse-form play directly into the
hands of a man drunk with words.

Semantic variation in *Pearl* is so rich as to defy ex-
haustive analysis. My impression is that almost any
group of stanzas would yield up the same kind of variations as do the first two stanzas, where the idea of the
uniqueness of the pearl is rendered in two ways:

> Ne proued I neuer her precios pere
>
> [4]

and

> I sette hyr sengeley in synglere;
>
> [8]

the related idea of her extreme beauty, in five ways:

> To clanly clos in golde so clere,
>
> [2]

> So rounde, so reken in vche araye,
>
> [5]

> So smal, so smoþe her sydeʒ were,
>
> [6]

> . . . þat pryuy perle wythouten spot,
>
> [12]

> My priuy perle wythouten spotte.
>
> [24]

Her special value to the speaker is rendered in seven
or eight ways at the same time by "my privy perle,"

and picked up again with great variety in the speaker's exclamation, "Allas! I leste hyr" (v. 9), his pining away, his love-longing, the heaviness of his heart, the swollen feeling in his breast, and the contrary feelings of pleasure, of hope, of reminiscence of former joy, of the silence, sweeter than song, when he thinks of her.

In the first two stanzas his losing of her is expressed in three variations:

> Allas! I leste hyr in on erbere,
>
> [9]
>
> Thurgh gresse to ground hit fro me yot,
>
> [10]
>
> . . . in þat spote hit fro me sprange;
>
> [13]

the variant motif of her being in the ground is itself varied, in the second and third stanzas, in yet four more ways:

> To þenke hir color so clad in clot,
>
> [22]
>
> O moul, þou marreȝ a myry iuele,
>
> [23]
>
> Þer such rycheȝ to rot is runne,
>
> [26]
>
> Þer hit doun drof in moldeȝ dunne;
>
> [30]

and a comparable set of variations grows up in the bouquet of herbs—spices, blooms, flowers, fruit, grass, wheat—that must follow the planting of *so semly a sede*. The image of the *sede* (v. 34) is itself the fourth (or perhaps the seventh) way that the poet has found to refer to her. When we go on to the fourth stanza we find along with new motifs some further resonations of those already introduced.

At the same time the refrain in the final lines linking the stanzas is making its turn of the phrase "perle wythouten spot"—and the word *spot*, according to the system already described, is picked up again in the first line of each stanza. Critics (particularly Wendell Stacy Johnson) have already shown how the poet revels in the ambiguity delivered into his hands by this sort of repetition, and how the play with language, here the variant meanings of *spot,* contributes to the sense of paradox, important to his meaning at this point: that the spotless pearl should be spotted, in the earth, and yet be perhaps without spot, without worldly location.[11]

We must pass reluctantly by the gorgeous verbal display of the second group of stanzas describing the dream-garden, in which the variation of the language seems particularly apt for rendering the glint and gleam of its "reflected brilliance" (in Johnson's phrase). But I cannot resist quoting one stanza:

> The dubbemente of þo derworth depe
> Wern bonkeʒ bene of beryl bryʒt.
> Swangeande swete þe water con swepe,
> Wyth a rownande rourde raykande aryʒt.
> In þe founce þer stonden stoneʒ stepe,
> As glente þurʒ glas þat glowed and glyʒt,
> As stremande sterneʒ, quen stroþe-men slepe,
> Staren in welkyn in wynter nyʒt;
> For vche a pobbel in pole þer pyʒt
> Watʒ emerad, saffer, oþer gemme gente,

Þat alle þe loȝe lemed of lyȝt,
So dere watȝ hit adubbement.

[109–120]

[The adornments of those splendid depths were fair
banks of bright beryl. Swirling sweetly the water did
sweep, flowing right on with a whispering sound. On the
bottom lay shining stones, that glowed and shimmered
like light through glass, and as streaming stars, when
earth-men sleep, shine in the heavens on a winter night.
For every pebble set there in the pool was an emerald,
sapphire, or precious gem, so that all the pool gleamed
with light, so precious was its splendor.]

The shimmering of the quality of this passage, if not
to be found in every section of the poem, is somehow
typical of it and of its meaning. The central meaning
of the *Pearl* symbolism is developed through variation
and reflection about a boldly repeated image which
gradually increases in richness as the poem progresses.[12]
The poem, in fact, is one of the most beautiful examples we have of the synthetic, accretive power of
symbolism, its capacity to bring together related significances into unitive simultaneous apprehension. The
poet who wrote

'O maskeleȝ perle in perleȝ pure,
Þat bereȝ,' quod I, 'þe perle of prys'

was not challenging us to figure out what the meaning
of the pearl is, but rather to appreciate the multiplicity
of meanings that the symbol could be made to inter-
relate: a girl, perhaps named Margery, a jeweler's precious stone fit for a prince; a kind of beauty such as
might be found in an earthly Paradise; an emblem of
moral purity; a sign of salvation; a badge of the company of the elect; a similitude of the kingdom of

Heaven; the gates of the New Jerusalem. Finally, the *precious perleȝ vnto his pay* of the poem's last line, where "he" is God, measures the range of meanings that have been traversed and linked up by the echo of the first line, with its simple-appearing *Perle, plesaunte to prynces pay.* It is no wonder, then, that in the course of the poet's rich unfolding of variant meanings for his central symbol, critics have felt impelled to reach for deeper and fuller significances in the dramatic action of the poem as a whole: to feel that the treatment of the speaker's personal loss, of the salvation of his little girl, and then of his own salvation, must also imply the problem of all mankind's loss of innocence and salvation, and the pearl's including in its significance the very soul of mankind.

Variation in the central symbol as the poem progresses is accompanied by a certain dramatics in the dialogue between the dreamer and the pearl-maiden, and here again we find a quality akin to that in the poem's poetics and symbolism. The relationship between the two speakers is curiously varied. Or rather, one had better say, the dreamer's felt relationship to the maiden is varied. For her attitude toward him is stable: a mixture of firm pedagogy and respectful sympathy, expressed even in the confident tone and rhythm of her speech. Here again we have sameness played against variation, and it functions (among other ways) to keep the elegiac pathos firmly in hand. One can begin to pick out the variations in the dreamer's view of the maiden simply by collecting some of the epithets he uses to refer to her. On first sight she is a *faunt,* a child (v. 161), and then a *mayden of menske, ful debonere* (162), then successively *þat gracios gay* (189), *þat frech as flor-de-lys* (195), *þat gyrle* (205),

þat precios pyece (229), that juel (253), þat damy-
selle (361), blysful (421), þat gaye (433), þat spe-
cyal spyce (938), þat lufly flor (962), my lyttel quene
(1147), my frely [beauty] (1155), and finally, after
the vision of her disappears, my perle (1173) again.

The dreamer's partial adoption of the stance of a
courtly lover is unmistakable here; it is supported by
such conventions as the garden setting, the elaborate
description of the lady, with her "vysayge whyt as
playn yuore [ivory]" (178) and her exquisite manners, who takes insufficient notice of luf-daungere (11)
[the power of love] and of his burning grief (387–
388). This stance is part of the poem's deep identification of Christian and courtly virtues, common also to
Sir Gawain and perhaps even more central to that
work. But we should not let the religious overtones of
the idea make us insensitive to the erotic, and to the
psychological penetration with which this variation of
the relationship is admitted into the poem. It is, of
course, one of several variations on the relationship
between father and daughter, man and pure maiden,
the living and the dead, that are by turns exposed to
us in their dialogue.

The psychological delicacy with which the meeting
is handled is prefigured in the dreamer's slight hesi-
tance in pursuing his way through the garden and in
his precarious mixture of fear and hope when he first
sees her. At his speechless wonder she respectfully
bows, like a daughter and also a lady, doffs her crown,
and greets him with *a lote lyȝte*, a glad sound (238).
But a moment later in response to his too ready complaint of his loss, she replaces her crown and soberly
corrects him. He excuses himself for the error, but the
rush of his affection and relief carry him into a second

error, his desire to live forever after with his pearl in the bright groves. This error elicits a certain impatience and shortness in her response:

> 'Jueler,' sayde þat gemme clene,
> 'Wy borde ȝe men? So madde ȝe be!'
>
> [289–290]

["Jeweler," said that clear gem, "Why do you men jest so? You are so mad!"]

The tone, surely, is that of a daughter who enjoys the privileges of a lady as well.

And so the conversation goes, the dreamer learning little by little to accept his loss as he accepts little by little the paradox of salvation, and making some more backward steps, some more errors, in progress. As soon as he has some intimation of his daughter's high estate he grows more humble, as might a countryman whose daughter had married a foreign prince. "Let's not argue now," says he "we see each other so seldom:"

> 'We meten so selden by stok oþer ston.
> Þaȝ cortaysly ȝe carp con,
> I am bot mol and manereȝ mysse.'
>
> [380–382]

["We see each other so seldom by tree or stone. Though you know how to speak courteously, I am just dust, and lack manners."]

But his humility leads him to another error; he does not quite understand how his little girl should have become a queen. A countess perhaps, yes:

> 'Of countes, damysel, par ma fay,
> Wer fayr in heuen to halde asstate

> Oþer elleȝ a lady of lasse aray;
> Bot a quene! Hit is to dere a date.'

[489–492]

["By my faith, young lady, it would be fine to have the position of countess in heaven, or else be a lady of lower rank. But a queen!—that is too high to reach."]

It is too high a mark for one so young. I emphasize the domestic and social overtones here at the expense of the theological point that is about to be expounded, but they are presented together, and if the former functions in the service of the latter, it never becomes purely metaphorical. Her reply—the parable of the vineyard—ends on a note of injury:

> 'Bot now þou moteȝ, me for to mate,
> Þat I my peny haf wrang tan here;
> Þou sayȝ þat I þat come to late
> Am not worþy so gret fere.'

[613–616]

["But now to contradict me you argue that I have taken my penny wrongly. You say that I that come too late am not worthy of such great fortune."]

Her tone of asperity sustains the emphasis given to the long passage of noble stanzas that follow, with their refrain:

> For þe grace of God is gret innoȝe.

At the end of the maiden's discourse, by far her longest in the poem, the dreamer is moved to the point of veneration of the queen before him and makes invocation to her. It is perhaps no accident that the pearl symbolism reaches its highest point of intensity here, in verses that we have already noticed:

'O maskeleʒ perle in perleʒ pure,
Þat bereʒ,' quod I, 'þe perle of prys. . . .'

[745–746]

The ensuing conversation serves to fill out the maiden's account of the state of the elect and the dreamer's glimpse of the New Jerusalem; their disagreement is forgotten. But the ambiguity of their relationship persists to the end. Mortal man's unfitness to conceive of the splendor of the New Jerusalem is mirrored in the dreamer's renewed sense of social humility, his reluctant presumption to ask yet another question:

'I schulde not tempte þy wyt so wlonc,
To Krysteʒ chambre þat art ichose.
I am bot mokke and mul among,
And þou so ryche a reken rose. . . .'

[903–906]

["I should not test your noble judgment—you who are chosen for Christ's bridal-chamber. I am just muck mixed together with dust, and you are so fair a fresh rose. . . ."]

But as the perspective lengthens in his vision of the procession of all the elect toward the throne of God, and he sees the maiden once again as one among many maidens, the old fatherly and loverly emotions are renewed:

I loked among his meyny schene
How þay wyth lyf wern laste and lade;
Þen saʒ I þer my lyttel quene
Þat I wende had standen by me in sclade.
Lorde, much of mirþe watʒ þat ho made
Among her fereʒ þat watʒ so quyt!

Þat syȝt me gart to þenk to wade
For luf-longyng in gret delyt.

[1145–1152]

[I looked among his shining troop, how they were loaded
and laden with life. Then there I saw my little queen that
I thought had stood near me in the valley. Lord, she was
rejoicing greatly, looking so white among her companions!
That sight made me decide to wade across, for love-
longing, in great delight.]

My lyttel quene . . . For luf-longyng in gret delyt:
almost the whole range of their relationship is compressed in those words. They give the last touch of
psychological rightness to the dreamer's final error: his
mad urge to cross the stream then and there, and his
consequent awakening out of his vision.

This awakening, the imperfection of the dreamer's
understanding and of his self-control, are essential to
the meaning of the poem, which comprehends here
something of the pathetic inadequacy of ordinary mortal thought and feeling to grasp the full nature of God's
love, God's grace, God's kingdom. The poem at its
end, as throughout in the maiden's discourse, and as
in the unity of its structure, never lets us doubt the
fullness and perfection of that kingdom; but through
its diction, style, and dramatics at the same time it
always makes us feel the variousness, the imperfection,
and the manifold partial intimations of it that we per-
ceive in this life.

Fullness, perfection, on the one hand, variousness,
imperfection, on the other—these motifs are just as
deeply involved in the style and meaning of *Sir Gawain and the Green Knight.* But the two are not the

same poem, and some of the same stylistic and structural traits in the serio-comic romance will be found to be supporting rather complex variants of the meanings we detect in the moral elegy.

The same rich synonymy and the same analytic, variational syntax supports in *Sir Gawain* much of the same subtly various and shimmering quality we find in *Pearl*. The daring white-on-white coloration of *Pearl* finds a suggestive parallel in the green-on-green of *Sir Gawain*. But as the various greens in *Sir Gawain* are often also mixed with some reds and golds, so the variety and fullness of detail which the style produces seems to support a greater sense of fecundity and, finally, of energy than in *Pearl*. The picture seems more crowded with detail, and if it indirectly hymns the manifold and various works of God, it also reflects a joy in the open-handedness and handiwork of men. The richness of the formal descriptions has often been noted. The armor of Sir Gawain, for example, is crowded with fringes and gold nailheads and gems, turtle-doves and true-love knots "so thickly embroidered as if many ladies had worked on it at home for seven years" (vv. 612–613). This sense of fullness of detail is picked up in the birds and butterflies and green stones and knots and bells that adorn the Green Knight and his horse, in the enticing costume of the lady of the castle, and even in the elaborate get-up of Morgan le Fay, "Toret and treieted [latticed] with tryflez aboute" (960). It is the same motive, I feel, and not wholly a faithfulness to late-fourteenth century architecture, that describes Bertilak's castle as having so many painted pinnacles scattered and clustered about it that it seemed pared out of paper (802). Very generally it is of a piece with the superlative feasts in the poem, full of music, double the usual number of dishes, with great variety of soups, fishes, and seasonings (189–197), and generously provided with leisure time and entertainment. Arthur's Christmas party lasts "ful fifteen dayes,"

With alle þe mete and þe mirþe þat men couþe avyse.
[45]

it is a world superlatively rich in content, even when the content is unpredictable or unfavorable to men, as in the splendidly concrete winter scenes, with their suggestion of a great multiplicity of hardships and adventures.[13]

As it expresses this sense of richness, fullness, and variety, the poem also generates a sense of superabundant energy. The description is itself one source of this feeling, for it either directly bespeaks the energy of fabulous handicraft, or that of nature. It is hard not to see in the Green Knight an overt symbolism of natural energy.[14] The vegetative associations of his appearance (the holly in his hand, his beard like a bush) would be enough to suggest it; but so do his size, his muscularity, and his manner both at Arthur's court and at the Green Chapel. When he is transformed into a country baron, the three hunting scenes superlatively perpetuate this symbolic role. But special energy is not reserved to the Green Knight; it is generated at every corner of the poem: obviously in the youth of Arthur and his guests, and in the martial reputation of Gawain. Less obviously but more profoundly in a widespread kinesthetic imagery, an imagery of muscular force, of tension and release, of the springing of steeds, the swinging of weapons, the exertion of grasping and leaping and catching, even of laughing, embracing and kissing. For even in the poem's quieter moments, the verbs seem to work overtime, possibly because of the continuous stretch that this poet applies to their meanings. So that between the hunting scenes, at bedtime in the castle,

> Vche burne to his bedde busked bylyue.
>
> [1411]

each man hurried to bed; the cock had *crowen* and *cakled* only three times when the lord *watz lopen* from his bed, and the company *dressed* to the wood before any daylight *sprenged*, to *chace*. While her husband is on his third hunt, the beautiful lady cannot sleep. She *ros hir vp radly* (1735), *comez* within the chamber door and *closes* it after her, *wayuez* open a window and *callez* on Gawain to wake up. The verbal energy persists even into the description of their general good cheer:

> With smoþe smylyng and smolt þay *smeten* into merþe,
> Þat al watȝ blis and bonchef þat *breke* hem bitwene
> . . .
> With luf-laȝyng a lyt he *layd* hym bysyde
> Alle the specheȝ of specialté that *sprange* of her mouthe.
>
> [1764–1765, 1777–1778]

[With pleasant and gentle smiles they fell into mirth, so that all was joy and happiness that broke out between them. . . . With a little affectionate laughter he parried all the provocative speeches that sprang from her mouth.]

This combined sense of superabundant fullness and energy—a sense not only of variety but of endless potentiality—always works in *Sir Gawain* in counterpoint with the extraordinary formalism to produce the total effect of the poem, which, like that of *Pearl,* is one of a surely-felt sense of order that nevertheless comprehends a great variety of experience. The contribution of the verse-form to this counterpoint is evident in the great freedom and variability of the alliterated main body of the stanza and the rather prim, delicate formality of the terminating rhymed bob-and-wheel that control and set it off.[15]

The Religion in *Sir Gawain* is by no means decorative or mechanical, but it is subordinated to the Courtesy, and although they remain versions of each other, it is the secular emphasis rather than the religious that is chiefly felt in the poem. So the order invoked by the poem is not chiefly that made by God, but rather the order made by men. It therefore requires no frame in a dream-vision of a better and higher world, but is rather framed by human history. The poem fittingly opens, then, with reference to the siege and the assault of Troy, that archetype of disaster, and continues with an account that is divided between the recitation of the subsequent successive foundings of Rome, Tuscany, Lombardy, and Britain—that is, successive restorations of order—and the reminder that Britain's building did not prevent the alternation of *werre and wrake and wonder,* and *blysse* and *blunder,* of the generation of bold men who loved strife and brought about *tene,* trouble, mischief. Many marvels have occurred here, continues the poet, and he will tell us concerning Arthur, the noblest king of all, something that he variously calls an *aunter in erde, a selly,* and *an outtrage awenture* (27–29).

The poet's variational structure, his synonymy here, three times brings into such close collocation historical events, marvel, and adventures as to suggest that the marvelous adventure to be narrated is not only historical (a forgivable poetic stance), but will constitute a comment on history and on the alternation between those two faces of history, *blysse and blunder,* that is, between order and confusion.[16] In a general sense the variational style in *Sir Gawain* supports and expresses a sense of variation—vicissitude—in human history.

The historical alternation between *blysse* and *blunder* is carried into the poem's pattern in many forms: *Sir Gawain* is much more a poem of contrasts and alternations than *Pearl.* But the thing to be primarily noted is that its alternations and contrasts, its moments of danger as well as of happiness, are all penetrated by a sense of ritual, caught up in a sense of pattern. It has been said that the three essentials of the festival spirit are that it involve excess, revelry; that it be affirmative, that it "say yes to life"; and that it display contrast, that it be the exceptional.[17] Correspondingly, the richness and energy which characterize the life of this festival poem are not merely decorative or celebratory, but rather pose the contrasting challenge of containment, of self-control, of rule, without which neither festivity nor civilization is possible.

Thus the vigorous action of the poem is intricately laced and bounded with dozens of variations of ritual, bargains, covenants, expressed or unspoken, which men make among themselves as an order in the world. The action is not only governed by social convention and formal agreements—that would be true of any society

poem—it is preoccupied with them. We see, furthermore, that a great deal of the aesthetic patterning of
the poem, of the unity of balanced and numerical repetitions, is a matter of social pattern, of ritual, custom,
or mutual agreement. Even the poet's mode of view-
ing the action, his way of describing scenes, is penetrated, as Marie Borroff has shown, by a sense of the
reciprocal.[18]

In this context we can take with maximum seriousness the recent suggestions in modern criticism that the
element of *game* in *Sir Gawain* is highly meaningful.[19]
For game is nothing other than a variation of the systems of covenants or agreements, the adopted sets of
rules, by which humans submit their energies and passions to limits and defend themselves from unruliness
and chaos.

The challenge of the Green Knight is at once an
adventure, a game, and a bargain; its full answer by
the hero Gawain is a test of his capacity to play the
game according to the bargain or the rules. The element of death that obtrudes loomingly in the midst of
this Christmas frolic and provides the romance with its
greatest dose of seriousness does nothing to diminish
the game going on. With the final laughter of Arthur's
court at the end and the revelation that, after all, sor-
cery and shape-shifting have been at work, the action
never loses completely its quality of play. We are never
sure, in fact, when the game leaves off and earnest
begins, for the game by itself has a serious import.

So many details of the poem fall into place in this
pattern that I can only indicate a few of them here.
That King Arthur has *ȝonge blod* and *brayn wylde*
(v. 89) is of course an element of the poem's energy,
its vitalism, which is carried out in the youthfulness of

his court and in the crowded and superlative quality of the feasting scene surrounding it. Energy is curbed and civilized at the same time by the nice sense of holiday ritual—it is a recognized occasion for revelry—and by the sense of courtesy and precedence that are observed throughout. The fact that Arthur's awaiting some *auenturus þyng, sum mayn meruayle,* some challenge *in iusting* (93–97) is itself a *custom* expresses precisely the dialectic we are tracing; and the fact that the Green Knight's challenge comes heralded by this custom has some effect on the way in which the poem's action accepts and contains that challenge. The mention of the challenge to jousting as among the possible adventures that Arthur awaits introduces some imagery that does more than prefigure the Green Knight's challenge; it perpetuates the notion of *reciprocity* that infuses the whole poem's sense of life and of play:

> To joyne wyth hym in iustyng, in jopardé to lay,
> Lede, lif for lyf, leue vchon oþer,
> As fortune wolde fulsun hom, þe fayrer to haue.
>
> [97–99]

> [To join with him in jousting, a man to stake life for life, each one to let the other have the fairer lot, as fortune might help him.]

The rules of the game could hardly have been better put. They have already been taken up in a lighter vein in the gift-giving game (with its payments in kisses, no doubt),[20] and I need not belabor this element in the bargain struck by Gawain with the rude stranger; it is this bargain, this game, with the system of reciprocal duties it entails, that forms the central action of the poem. It is perhaps worth noting, however, the words used by the Green Knight to describe it: *þe gomen* [game] (273), *a Crystemas gomen* (283), *oure for-wardes* [agreement] (378), *þe couenaunt* (393), and the solemnity with which Gawain is sworn to recipro-cate. "Game" and "solemn agreement" are synony-mous.

The splendid description of the passage of the sea-sons—with its play on change, variety, growth, and decay, all encircled by natural law (vv. 500–533)—is entirely in harmony with the structure we are fol-lowing. The ritualism of the arming of Gawain and the description of his shield invoke the norms of chival-ric and Christian behavior which are part of the rules of the game; and of the same significance, and even more prominent, are the rules of the game of love and courtesy which come to the fore at Bertilak's castle. The richness of the poem's morality is that all of these are great games, great systems, and that Gawain must play all of them, consummately, at the same time.

The motif of the exchange of gifts intensifies the complexity and the difficulty of the test that Gawain undergoes. Most obviously, it obliges him to reveal his favors from the lady and thus makes concealment of the girdle an overt fault, an act of *vntrawþe,* perfidy. It also reinforces on an apparently sportive, inconse-quential level the motif of reciprocity and of covenant which is at the heart of the deeper, life-and-death action:

'Ʒet firre,' quoþ þe freke, 'a forwarde we make:
Quat-so-euer I wynne in þe wod hit worþez to
    yourez,
And quat chek so Ʒe acheue chaunge me þerforne.
Swete, swap we so, sware with trawþe,

Queþer, leude, so lymp, lere oþer better.'
'Bi God,' quoþ Gawayn þe gode, 'I grant þertylle,
And þat yow lyst for to layke, lef hit me þynkes.'
'Who bryngez vus þis beuerage, þis bargayn is
    maked.' . . .

And efte in her bourdyng þay bayþen in þe morn
To fylle þe same forwardez þat þay byfore maden:
Wat chaunce so bytydez hor cheuysaunce to
    chaunge,
What nwez so þay nome, at naȝt quen þay metten.
Þay acorded of þe couenauntez byfore þe court alle.
                    [1105–1112, 1404–1408]

["Furthermore," said the man, "let us make an agreement: whatever I win in the woods will be yours, and for
that, exchange with me whatever advantage you get. Fine
sir, let's make the swap and give our words, whether we
lose or come out better." "By God," said good Gawain,
"I agree to it; it delights me that you want to play." "The
bargain will be made as soon as someone brings us a
drink." . . . And again in their jesting they agreed in the
morning to fulfill the same bargain that they made before:
no matter what might befall, to exchange their winnings,
whatever new things they got, when they met at night.
They agreed to the covenant before the whole court.]

For the poet to have balanced the love scenes and
love tokens with the scenes and the prizes of the hunt
seems tonally and thematically perfect. The hunting
scenes are neither decorative nor excrescent nor even
overdeveloped. For the hunt (pursuit of game) is a
game of a most ancient and vital form, and by describing these lively chases the poet in the first place powerfully perpetuates the poem's sense of wild energy,
barely to be controlled by the rules and custom of the
hunt. It is surely the function of describing the careful

dismemberment of the deer and boar to reestablish the sense of ritual order after the vital rush of the hunt itself. The envelopment of each love scene between the halves of a hunting scene put beyond doubt an artistic intention. Professor Savage long ago suggested some analogies between the character of the lady's quarry and that of Bertilak's, with the capping observation that on the third day Gawain acts the fox in the bedroom as the hunters hunt the fox in the field.[21] Surely a prior poetic relevance is in the fact of the hunts themselves. It will perhaps trivialize my point—but clarify it nevertheless—to quote a bit of Chaucer here:

> She was so propre and sweete and likerous
> I dar wel seyn, if she hadde been a mous,
> And he a cat, he wolde hire hente anon.
> [*Miller's Tale*, 3345–3347]

The poet knew, as we know, that the game of dalliance and love-talk is the containing and civilizing of animal sexuality. Our sense of Gawain's being tested is intensified, then, not only by the seductive charm of the lady, but by the imagery of the chase, of natural energy, deeply masculine, deeply sensory, with which the hunts surround his temptation and almost promise to validate his taking the lady. The life-and-death struggles of the hunted animals, finally, are played against Gawain's risk of his own life. If the lord's brutal courage in the face of the boar underlines the touch of prudence in Gawain, the deaths of the animals and the counterpointed vitality of the lord do in fact help to extenuate (if not validate) the love for life which motivates Gawain's one act of *untrawþe*. We can see in this perspective, indeed, how the felt vitality, the festive "saying of yes to life" in the whole poem's imagery and style, finally enters deeply into the poem's moral significance.

To turn back again to the theme of covenant and reciprocity, we may observe that the crucial dialogue between Gawain and the lady is embedded in a web of preliminary *exchanges*. There is the context of the exchange of general courtesies in the castle; the exchange of wit and compliment which constitutes their love dialogues; and such small but suggestive variations of the theme of chivalric rules as her suggestion of a military truce as she captures him on the first morning, and his refusal to countenance on the second morning a kiss taken by force, *geuen not with goud wylle* (1500).

The ending of the third dialogue is literally *about* exchange and reciprocity. The lady requests a gift, a token, in remembrance (1799). And Gawain's replies are politely ambiguous. He is unhappily not provided with baggage full of precious gifts; but he makes clear that while the lady deserves the most precious token of her hospitality—something he can and should reciprocate—it would not be right, it would not be to her honor, to give her a token for *drurye,* for love (1805). That, it is clear, would be a false token of reciprocity. The lady reverses the terms and offers him the gift of a ring. He refuses it and then refuses the green girdle on the same grounds:

"I haf none yow to norne [offer], ne noȝt wyl I take."
[1823]

His final acceptance and keeping of the girdle stands out from the poem's tight weaving of mutual exchange and agreements, not only as the only violation of his pledge with Bertilak, but as the only reward accepted without fair exchange given.

The rhetoric and imagery of ungrudging reciprocity, answering, unflinching truth to one's covenants, is very strong in the final episode, and I have of course passed over a great many other incidental examples of it in this discussion. The churlish behavior of Gawain's guide functions both to set off the ignorance of those (churls) who do not understand the world of covenants and to underline the terror of a state in which no such civilized restraints exist. The churl's picture of the Knight of the Green Chapel is of a monster unreasonable and uncontrollable, whose only occupation is slaughter—even of innocuous priests. In the face of the churl's terror, Gawain's reply is to invoke the ultimate covenant, that between man and God, and ride on alone.

Gawain's most obvious moral test is the test of chastity in the castle, which is presented less in and for itself than as a test, rather, of *trawþe* to the rules of hospitality.

He cared for his cortaysye, lest craþayn he were,
And more for his meschef ȝif he schulde make synne,
And be traytor to þat tolke þat þat telde aȝt.
[1773–1775]

[He was concerned about his courtesy, lest he should be boorish, and even more about the trouble he would be in if he committed a sin, and betrayed the man who owned that house.]

But this test is only preliminary to the confrontation at the Green Chapel, which, precisely because it has no doctrinal content but consists in naked adherence to the covenant itself—because it is, in fact, the final inning or period in a Christmas game—is the deepest test of all. The poem seems to exemplify precisely what Huizinga means in *Homo Ludens* when he says: "The play concept as such is of a higher order than seriousness. For seriousness seeks to exclude play, whereas play can very well include seriousness."[22]

Much as in *Pearl*, *Sir Gawain* contains a strong sense of the ideal, delights in the variations from it, and ends with a tolerant sense of the difficulties of perfection. Even Eneas, *þe trewest on erthe*—the poet has reminded us—was once tried for treachery.[23] As in the *Pearl*, the style and structure of the poem are based on a deep interplay between formal unity and variation. *Sir Gawain* is the larger and more complex poem, its setting is more social than private, and it gives greater emphasis to the notions of disorder and of the imperfectness of human arrangements than does *Pearl*, so we might naturally expect to find in it a more suggestive connection with the sensibility of its own time. And in a sense we do. *Sir Gawain*, which is about *trawþe* and faithfulness in men, may be implying more about treachery and churlishness in its own culture than *Pearl* suggests about religious scepticism and the capitulation to grief. But the poems seem to me nevertheless more alike than different. The man who wrote these poems cannot have been ignorant, unobservant, or insensitive, and the times cried aloud for a reassertion of faith in God and in the integrity of men. The variational style in *Pearl* images precisely the imperfection of man's vision of the divine perfection. In *Gawain* the style supports the poem's sense of fecundity, but also its sense of vicissitude, of disruptive energy, of the inconsistency and surprise that attend human affairs. But in both poems the extraordinary integrity of form, the sense that the variations are variations from an ideal order, continually asserts the primacy of that order. We come in each poem to a vision acutely aware of man's imperfection but unshakably confident in his religious and chivalric ideals.

If the *Pearl* poet is responding to the troubles of his times, his response, especially in the two masterpieces, is mostly oblique. Crisis touches him, no doubt profoundly, but in these poems it is completely absorbed in his art. Indeed, the richness of the poems combined with their artistic purity, the self-containment of their meaning, the sublime control and assurance with which they are composed, the total poetic energy they absorb, suggest a man for whom the perfection of his art has become a kind of defense against crisis. Each of the two poems is composed of exactly one hundred and one stanzas, and I take that extra stanza in each case to be a sign of humility. But it is the humility of an inveterate artificer. The *Pearl* poet has been compared as a writer to George Herbert, to Gerard Manley Hopkins, and to James Joyce, and there are good reasons for each comparison. But I like even better the observation made by one of my students not long ago, that for his time he is very much like the late Wallace Stevens: a "cubist" artist, with a fractionating, variational vision; and as artist, totally an artist—immersed in an age of crisis, but somehow beyond it, refining out through his art almost all of its accidental qualities, rendering finally, through form, only its shimmer, its beauty, and its moral essence.

III

PIERS PLOWMAN:
THE POETRY OF CRISIS

IN THE LAST TWO DECADES PIERS PLOWMAN HAS BEEN
the object of concentrated attention by an impressive
array of scholar-critics. Impressive not so much in their
gross number, for there are many more investigators
of Chaucer, for instance; but relative to its bulk and
complexity, the poem has attracted extraordinary resources of talent to its elucidation. Unlike the works of
the *Pearl* poet, it is not at all a modern discovery. It
survives in over fifty manuscripts, making it one of the
best sellers of the English Middle Ages, and it has been
well known and a focus of theological, social, and
scholarly controversy ever since. But as with *Pearl* and
Sir Gawain, modern criticism (along with modern textual scholarship) has added a full new dimension to
the study of the poem, and that consists of nothing
other than regarding it *as* a poem. Recent investigators
have been notable for a complexity of equipment that
answers the complexity of the task: an acute awareness
of the textual problems, a deepening understanding of
the theology of the time, a broad knowledge of medieval literature, and an appreciation of artistic form and
poetic language. A respect and love for the artist himself is axiomatic; in addition, some have been able to
bring to their studies a personal religious commitment
which makes it possible for them to accept the meaning
of the poetry with total sympathy, simultaneously as
art and as faith.[1]

In terms of equipment and of sympathy, then, much of what we have to bring to bear on the study of the poem has in fact been brought to bear in recent years. Of course this is not all we shall ever have. Our knowledge of fourteenth-century culture is still notoriously sketchy; and we can look forward to the completion of the reediting of the text, which is now in progress, and to advances all along the line. But I advert, perhaps ponderously, to the impressiveness of what has been done, to the learning, ingenuity, insight, and sympathy that have been lavished upon the work, to suggest the validity of the results of modern criticism—namely, its extraordinary inconclusiveness—and the validity of the meaning of those results: that *Piers Plowman* must in important ways *be* inconclusive; that its form and style are symptomatic of some sort of breakdown.

The problem with which *Piers Plowman* confronts us has been variously expressed by its most sympathetic critics. "Surely the starting point," George Kane writes, "is this paradox of total greatness and local failures"; and his essay goes a long way toward explaining the paradox without removing it. A. C. Spearing speaks of an "effect of potent vagueness" as being typical of the poem. Morton Bloomfield speaks of "a basic uncertainty" in Langland's mind. John Lawlor finds "penetrating clarity and largeness of vision . . . side by side with the very taste of purposelessness." Elizabeth Salter and Derek Pearsall attempt mightily to account for "the apparent inconclusiveness and deviousness of the poem's movement"; they describe the reading of the poem as "an experience . . . both richer and, at times, more confusing than any analysis or abstract can suggest."[2]

The puzzling quality of the poem is thus widely felt,

and variously located, and one is forced to observe that despite our real advances in knowledge, modern criticism does not dispel one's sense of puzzlement, but rather tends to substitute new and more complex puzzles for the old. Thus in sharing the modern concern with the problem of the poem's art, we must nevertheless recognize that older questions—the question of authorship, for instance, and the question of the "thought" of the poem—have now been subsumed in the problems of the poem's form, structure, and coherence, which virtually all modern critics recognize.

Medieval literary theory does not lean heavily on the ideas of form, structure, and coherence, preferring rather to dwell on the methods of amplification and ornamentation, which in too many cases obliterate form and structure. But general aesthetic theory is full of the awareness of proportion, order, and composition in art.[3] In any case the medieval poet, no matter how unsophisticated his aesthetic, had numerous other occasions for controlling his form or structure. In religious poetry there was always the clarity of form imposed by theology, by belief itself. A highly rationalized and numerical theology and a belief in the significance of formal or typological correspondences will help to produce an ordered and rationally divided work: if on God, then on his three aspects; if on the afterlife, then divided into Hell, Purgatory, and Paradise; if on penitence, then dealing successively with the four stages: repentance, confession, satisfaction, absolution.

Gothic art derives formal characteristics from related but more general habits of thought. The emergence in the twelfth century of dialectic as the chief method in philosophical exposition does not originate but only caps and gives final validation to a deep-seated formal tendency in the Gothic mind, a tendency which shapes whole classes of poems: *conflictus, tenson,* debate, the body and soul, the knight and the clerk, the Owl and the Nightingale, Winner and Waster.

Another Gestalt that is most congenial to Gothic art is that of the procession, the linear progression through stages or stations, as in a journey. It can be used in describing the succession of bays, leading to the altar, in the nave of the Gothic cathedral. In the other arts it can be found everywhere from the Bayeux tapestry to the procession of the mystery plays. It is a formal or structural factor in the *Divine Comedy* and the *Decameron.* As the pilgrimage it underlies the *Canterbury Tales* and many a moral allegory; as the quest it is the formal basis of much in romance.

Finally, the traditions and conventions of genre provide formal directions for the conduct of the poem: the dream-vision, the allegory, the romance, the fabliau, the sermon, each has accepted characteristics which contribute to form and structure.

The first thing to be observed about Langland is that although his work bears traces of almost all the large formal resources I have mentioned, it is finally controlled and explained by none of them.

There have been impressive attempts to discover a theological architecture of the poem. These attempts were for a long time focussed on what seems to be a perfectly clear and typically medieval division of its concerns into four parts. The full, completed poem consists of a "Vision of William Concerning Piers the Plowman," being about a third of the whole, and then a series of visions concerning "Do-Well, Do-Better, and Do-Best." What could be clearer? The initial vision should be an introduction describing the problem, the present ills of society, and the successive sections Do-Well, Do-Better, and Do-Best should treat of successively higher levels of right conduct. But beyond this all remains cloudy. The poet is not consistent in his use of the terms "Dowel, Dobet, and Dobest the third." He uses them often enough—one critic has called them "a kind of maddening refrain,"[4]—but we do not know what they mean. We could linger for the rest of our discussion with the theories on this one point: that Dowel, Dobet, and Dobest are the active life, the contemplative life, and the episcopal life; that they refer to the purgative, illuminative, and unitive stages of mystical contemplation; that they deal with the gifts to Man of, respectively, God, Christ, and the Holy Spirit;[5] and so on.

One sympathetic and remedial suggestion is that the multiplicity of possible meanings of the three ways of life is intentional, and that any and all may be present.[6] A related view is that each of the successive meanings of the three lives somehow augments the others.[7] More pessimistic is the observation that apart from one passage in Passus XIX, and in the manuscript rubrics, references to the triad all come in the Do-well section "and nowhere else, and that there the three Do's are defined in six or seven different ways."[8] Other critics have turned from the schema completely, suggesting that the poem does not operate on a conceptual structure at all, and may even be explicitly rejecting "the method of precise intellectual distinction."[9] Taken together, the best criticism of the poem suggests that what might have been a great tripartite medieval structure does not rise here, or at least that it is neither clearly outlined nor solidly based.

Turning now to other major possible sources of

coherence, we find similar difficulties. *Piers Plowman* is really too long to be a debate as such, but the several dialogues between the Dreamer and interlocutors, as well as doses of dualistic and antithetic structure, give us some suggestion that its essential organization might be dialectical. This suggestion is very strong at the beginning, where the narrator, clothed as a hermit, is wandering on the Malvern Hills, falls asleep by a brook, and dreams that he is in a wilderness. High in the east, toward the sun, he sees a beautiful tower on a hilltop, and beneath it, in a deep dale, a dungeon. In between is a fair field full of folk, busy about all the activities of the world (Prologue, vv. 1–19). That this tower and dungeon, the high hill and dark dale, represent opposite alternatives, Jerusalem and Babylon, Heaven and Hell, would be a normal inference for allegorical poems. This inference is confirmed when, after an extended description of the fair field full of folk, in Passus I a beautiful lady named Holy Church instructs the Dreamer, telling him that the tower is the tower of Truth (or God) and the dungeon is the dwelling of Wrong (or the Devil). The conversation between Holy Church and the Dreamer is reminiscent of that of a host of other pairs of figures in medieval dialogue. Sometimes such figures engage in equal debate (which has been called "horizontal" debate), as in the *Owl and the Nightingale*. At other times they take the "vertical" roles of master and pupil, as in Boethius' *Consolation* or in *Pearl*. The forms can be combined, as in the second part of the *Roman de la Rose,* which is a horizontal debate among the various exponents of love, but has a vertical character in that each one successively takes the part of a master instructing the Dreamer (or Bel Acueil). Here in *Piers Plow-*

man the debate or dialogue is vertical. After Holy Church instructs the Dreamer concerning Truth and charity, in Passus II she points out to him another beautiful lady, clad in scarlet and jewels, named in the poem Meed; she is the daughter of False, as Holy Church is the daughter of God, and when Holy Church departs we expect the Whore of Babylon to have *her* turn in the dialogue that seems to be developing.

But Langland, in then going on with an extensive treatment of some of the evils of the world, wanders *out* of the dialectical genre framework thus established. Instead of sermon or polemic by Meed, he writes a semidramatic allegory on the relations between Meed and Falsehood, and Meed and Conscience, in a setting explicitly named the English court at Westminster (Passus III and IV). The following section of the poem shows Reason or Conscience preaching to the people, bringing on Repentance and the confessions of the Seven Deadly Sins (Passus V). Thus, in turn, the three or four-part pattern of the stages of Penitence temporarily becomes the organizing principle of the poem, and this in turn soon merges with the pilgrimage form. Confession over, the poet has a moving vision of the throng of repentant sinners inspired to seek Truth, but not knowing the way. Here for the first time enters Piers or Peter, a simple plowman, who gives the simple prescription of a life of honest work and doing good—doing the work that God has cut out for one—as the way to Truth. Piers is conceived here as a guide on a pilgrimage; but the plowman's pilgrimage is to plow his half-acre. After dealing with the problems of man's laziness and malingering, the poet shows Truth sending to Piers and his followers a pardon and a promise of eternal life (Passus VII).

Thus ends the first part—possibly to be called the Introduction—of the poem. The vision which follows shows us the narrator in lonely quest of Dowel. If the dialectical structure seems to have dropped out of sight, we might rediscover it in the series of debates in which the Dreamer now engages with such figures as Thought, Wit, Studie, Ymagynatyf, and Conscience. There are enough of these debates to establish that Langland set great store by the form. But in the final analysis the poem does not *proceed* by means of them. On the one hand, the Dreamer never finds, as a pupil in his "vertical" debates, any master with whose teaching he seems finally consoled. The multiplicity of subsequent masters, as Bloomfield has noted,[10] casts some shadow even on the role of Holy Church. She never reappears in the poem, although, paradoxically, it is surely her teaching which comes closest finally to providing what resolution the poem contains. Nor is Piers the Plowman, the most authoritative figure in the poem, ever brought into true dialogue with the Dreamer. Meanwhile, as Rosemary Woolf has said, "There is no poetic resolution to the opposing arguments" in the debates; "they are merely accumulated and put on one side."[11]

The quest pattern as the formal basis of the poem has an impressive number of supporters; but there is a serious issue whether the quest is effective artistically, that is, as a formal device in the poem, or biographically, that is, as a way of looking at the life of the poet, of which the poem itself is a record or symptom. The quest pattern reappears now and again in the poem, with the Dreamer ever seeking instruction on the means of salvation or perfection, but it is so distorted by digressions and alterations that its literary status is open to doubt. It is a quest that has many beginnings, no middle, and an ambiguous end; the quest leads back to where it started, in a pathetically hopeful vision of the human Conscience vowing to become a pilgrim to "walk wide as the world lasts to seek Piers the Plowman," destroyer of Pride. We cannot demand a compulsive neatness from medieval poets, nor impeccable theology or logic. But we expect to recognize some form, some control; if the poem is a quest, a spiritual autobiography, it is like none other of its time.

Sympathetic criticism of the poem as quest has tended toward accepting its incoherencies, somehow, as part of its art. Langland saw the Dreamer's quest, say Elizabeth Salter and Derek Pearsall, "as a search for truth which was complex, often contradictory, and cumulative." In successive bouts with the same problem these critics point out at least six searches in the poem, which exist neither in simple sequence nor in isolation, but which, they assert, "can be gradually or dramatically revealed as similar, even identical in direction and end-point." We must agree that all the searches in the poem are for Truth, early designated by Holy Church as the best of treasures, and the object of Piers Plowman's pilgrims. But in describing the literary relations of the successive journeys *in the poem,* the critics fall back on comparisons that suggest abandonment of a literary conception of form for something like real life. The searches, they say, "unfold out of the first search in a way which is more like a process of organic growth than deliberate literary design."[12] George Kane grasps the thorns more boldly:

> Indeed the figure of a search affords an excellent analogy for the progress of the poem; the false starts and changes of direction, frequent pauses, anxieties,

hesitations and impatience which characterize it are
thus excellently illustrated.[13]

This comes close to invoking the fallacy of imitative
form; and many a reader has felt that the poem more
than merely *represents* "the false starts and changes of
direction, frequent pauses, anxieties, hesitations, and
impatience" of the search for Truth. It not only represents them, it contains them; the reader or audience not
only appreciates them, he suffers them, and it is not
surprising that more than one critic, coming to a point
of temporary resolution or of clarity in the text, sounds
as if he is sharing the Dreamer's joy and relief. "So the
Plowman, and after him the Saviour Himself, are sent
to meet our need," says John Lawlor, who makes of
the reading itself a necessary experience "of the very
sense of weariness and apparent purposelessness that
any stage of the journey may afford."[14]

We find this kind of difficulty and this kind of solution again if we look at the other resources of literary
genre that were open to the poet. The poem can be
regarded as a series of dreams or visions in allegorical
form, but it is neither vision nor allegory in the conventional sense. Its deviations from the traits of genre,
indeed, give us some positive indications of the ultimate quality of the poet's vision and of his historical
significance.

The medieval vision—very early a vehicle for
describing the afterlife—is conventionally adapted for
the description of experience on a level other than that
of everyday sensation. Resting firmly on the authority
of biblical visions (Ezekiel, Daniel, St. John) and on
a well-developed science of dreams, it was so natural
a vehicle for the wonderful that even the love-poets

took it up as a frame for their erotic heavens, hells, and purgatories. Both the Bible and dream-science taught that the dream or vision could be of hidden significance, and this very early led to a solid merger between dream and allegory. Allegory, highly developed in the Middle Ages as a device to explore the world of noumena—of nonsensuous moral and psychological entities—creates precisely that appearance of the strange and wonderful—of cryptic, nonnaturalistic, needing-to-be-interpreted experience—for which the dream-vision is the natural frame. Allegory has its own inner laws, chief of which is that it is habitually telling two simultaneous stories. One is fictional, rendered by the interplay of personified abstractions—like Charity and Cupidity, who may be rendered as two attractive ladies who struggle for the attention of a young man named Free Will. The other story is the simultaneous, hidden signification—let us say a moral issue in the actual world or even a crisis in the mind of a single person. The characteristic allegory keeps the two stories separate and distinct, that there be no confusion between the two worlds or two levels of reality represented. Medieval poets vary in their capacity to manage allegory, but by the time Langland wrote, the allegorical dream-vision was a venerable medieval genre whose form and tradition were known to everyone.

Langland introduces his dream-vision conventionally, with good heart, and he arouses conventional expectations. The time is May, the narrator wanders forth in the world to hear wonders; a marvel befell him, he says, almost a fairy-tale. He dreamt a marvelous dream, that he was in a wilderness; then comes mention of the allegorical tower and dungeon, and we seem indeed to have been introduced to a strange, allegorical world. But Langland makes no attempt to sustain either the sense of unfamiliarity, strangeness, or wonder sanctioned by the dream-form, nor can he for more than a few moments maintain the sense of the separateness of different levels of reality suggested by allegory. To put it another way, for him the familiar London scene is a wilderness seen in a vision. The world of moral abstractions is concrete and present, and the concrete, present, everyday world is itself an allegory, heavy with moral significance.

Turning to a description of the fair field full of folk —an allegory of the present condition of man in the world—he cannot render it schematically or abstractly, as in a vision, although he tries. "Some men put themselves to the *plow*" he says "and they played very seldom. In tilling and sowing they worked very hard, and earned what wasters destroy with gluttony. And some put themselves to *pride,* and appareled themselves accordingly; they came all decked out in the disguises of clothing." Right there in the forceful parallel between the concrete term "plow" and the abstract term "pride," as if there were not the slightest difference in kind between them, we have a small hint of the nature of Langland's vision: "plow" for him is a general moral term, "pride" is a concrete reality.[15] As his summary of the activities of man proceeds we can detect his impatience with allegory and even with mimetics. As abstraction and concreteness alternate or merge in his discourse so do the graphic and the doctrinal, description and exhortation.

Were it not too long a tale, I could tell how, again and again, Langland's sense of the present reality rends the curtain of allegory. How he brings abstractions like Meed, Reason, and Conscience before such historical figures as King Edward III at Westminster; how, in the midst of an allegorical pleading between Meed and Conscience before the King, another and much more concrete case suddenly comes up: Peace vs. Wrong. The episode amplifies for us the nature of Meed (Lucre), but its realism and color take us deep into a specific neighborhood (Passus IV, 47–109). Wrong has stolen Peace's wife, ravished a girl named Margaret, and also Rose (Reginald's sweetheart), has stolen geese and little pigs, broken the barn door and taken grain; he has even beaten up Peace and seduced his maid. Having—allegorically—the King's ear, Langland cannot refrain from inveighing against these deplorably literal results of the system of Maintenance in the countryside.

In illustration of Langland's curious way with dream-allegory I will only mention in addition his celebrated treatment of the Seven Deadly Sins. This sequence stands for a step in the process of Penance: Confession is represented by a series of confessions made by personifications of the sins. But the sins are not equal personifications, nor are their performances the least bit uniform. The names, again, are significant. Envy is called Envy, but Lechery is called Lecher (a degree less of abstraction), and Pride, even less abstractly, is represented as a girl named Peronelle Proud-Heart. Covetousness is called Sir Harvey. When Langland comes to the "confession" of Gluttony, local realism takes over completely. Glutton on his way to confession meets Betty the brewer and he is led into the tavern instead.

We have a tavern scene comparable to this in an early thirteenth-century French moral allegory, the *Songe d'Enfer,* where the Dreamer, having passed

through the city of Covetousness and crossed the River
of Gluttony, comes to the tavern and is welcomed by
Theft. He gambles and meets with characters named
Gambling, False Count, and Cheating. Then Drunkenness enters with her son Brawling, who has a fight
with the Dreamer. Drunkenness takes the Dreamer via
Fornication on to the brothel, which harbors Larceny
and Shame, the daughter of Sin. The conduct of this
earlier work is allegorically conventional and impeccable of its kind. These are the characters, and this the
action we expect to find in such a setting. Although
the author (like Dante) is fond of peppering his account with the names of actual people and places, such
references are kept firmly within the boundaries of the
moral-allegorical frame. (Thus Gambling asks the
Dreamer for news of one Michiel de Treilles, but he
is not confused with nor does he give up his role to the
apparently notorious Michiel.) Langland's tavern, on
the other hand, is incurably concrete and local:

> Thanne goth Glotoun in and grete othes after;
> Cesse the souteresse sat on the benche,
> Watte the warner and his wyf bothe,
> Tymme the tynkere and tweyne of his prentis,
> Hikke the hakeneyman and Hughe the nedeler,
> Clarice of Cokkeslane and the clerke of the cherche,
> Dawe the dykere and a dozeine other;
> Sire Piers of Pridie and Peronelle of Flaundres,
> A ribibour, a ratonere, a rakyer of Chepe,
> A ropere, a redyngkyng, and Rose the dissheres,
> Godfrey of Garlekehithe, and Gryfin the Walshe,
> And vpholderes an hepe erly bi the morwe
> Geuen glotoun with glad chere good ale to hansel.
>
> [B V 314–326]

There was laughyng and louryng and 'let go the
    cuppe,'
And seten so til euensonge and songen vmwhile,
Tyl Glotoun had y-globbed a galoun an a Iille.
His guttis gunne to gothely as two gredy sowes;
He pissed a potel in a *pater-noster*-while,
And blew his rounde ruwet at his rigge-bon ende,
That alle that herde that horne held her nose after,
And wissheden it had be wexed with a wispe of firses.
    He myȝte neither steppe ne stonde er he his staffe
        hadde;
And thanne gan he go liche a glewmannes bicche,
Somme tyme aside and somme tyme arrere,
As who-so leyth lynes forto lacche foules.
    And whan he drowgh to the dore thanne dymmed
        his eighen,
He stumbled on the thresshewolde an threwe to the
    erthe.
Clement the cobelere cauȝte hym bi the myddel,
For to lifte hym alofte and leyde him on his knowes;
Ac Glotoun was a gret cherle and a grym in the
    liftynge,
And coughed vp a caudel in Clementis lappe;
Is non so hungri hounde in Hertford schire
Durst lape of the leuynges so vnlouely thei smauȝte.
    With al the wo of this worlde his wyf and his
        wenche
Baren hym home to his bedde and brouȝte hym
    therinne.
And after al this excesse he had an accidie,
That he slepe Saterday and Sonday til sonne ȝede
    to reste.
Thanne waked he of his wynkyng and wiped his
    eyghen;

The fyrst worde that he warpe was, 'where is the bolle?'

[B V 344–367]

[Then Glutton went in and Great Oaths after him. Cis the shoemaker sat on the bench, Wat the game-keeper and his wife also, Tim the tinker and two of his apprentices, Hick the horse-renter and Hugh the needle-maker, Clarice of Cock's Lane and the clerk of the church, Davy the ditch-digger and a dozen others, Sir Piers the priest and Peronelle the Flemish whore, a fiddler, a rat-catcher, a Cheapside street-cleaner, a rope-maker, a horse-boy, and Rose the dish-seller, Godfrey of Garlickhithe and Griffin the Welshman, and a bunch of auctioneers, early in the morning, hospitably gave Glutton a drink of good ale for luck. . . .

There was laughing and scowling and "Let go the cup," and they sat there till vespers, singing a while, till Glutton had gulped down more than a gallon. His guts began to rumble like two greedy sows. He pissed two quarts as quickly as you could say the Lord's Prayer, and blew the round bugle at the end of his backbone so that all who heard that horn held their noses afterwards, and wished it had been stoppered with a bunch of furze.

He could neither walk nor stand till he had his staff, and then he moved like a (blind) minstrel's bitch, sometimes sideways and sometimes backwards, like someone laying nets to catch birds. And when he drew near the door his eyesight dimmed; he stumbled on the sill and fell to the earth. Clement the cobbler grabbed him by the middle to lift him up, and he got him to his knees. But Glutton was a big fellow, terribly heavy to lift, and he threw up a mess right in Clement's lap. There isn't a hound in Hertfordshire hungry enough to lap up those leftovers, they smelled so foul.

With a world of trouble his wife and his maid carried him home and got him to bed. And after all this carousing he fell into such a stupor that he slept all through Saturday and Sunday until sunset. Then he waked out of his

sleep and wiped his eyes. The first words that he got out
were "Where's the cup?"]

After the confessions of the sins, a few pages farther
on, appears Repentance, to whom Langland entrusts
one of his most lofty and touching utterances on the
meaning of Christ's sacrifice—and the religious allegory is resumed until its next interruption.

Langland's unorthodox form and genre—if form
and genre they be—produce a final structural quality
I want to mention: that is a peculiarity in his sense of
locus or space. For while the poem goes ahead by
seemingly ordinary chronology—in seven successive
visions, with wakings in between, and with liberal use
of the formula "and then,"—the location of its characters and actions and their spatial relations are con-
tinuously shifting.[17]

Of course we do not ask for a realistic landscape
from dream-vision; nor do the materials of allegory—
the moral and psychological entities—have natural
spatial relations. Yet partly because of the logical and
temporal relations among these moral and psychological entities, partly because of the device of personifica-
tion, and partly because narrative itself connotes space
as well as time, medieval visions and allegories do generate a considerable geometry and often an elaborate
geography. The allegory as pilgrimage—the genre to
which *Piers Plowman* is closest—involves a strong
sense of location and space, and this is often turned to
advantage in the allegory itself. It makes things clearer.
In the *Pèlerinage de Vie Humaine*, a fourteenth-century
French work of the genre, the geography is governed
by the relations of the concepts dealt with. The
Dreamer-pilgrim comes to a fork in the road; on the

left is Laziness, on the right Work, and his body coun-
sels him to take the path of Laziness, which he does.
His well-wishers, Grace and Reason, tell him to leave
this road and come to the other through the hedge
planted by Penitence. As he is trying to find a way
through the hedge, he is attacked by sins—and so
forth.[18] Not a very subtle or complicated matter, no
doubt, but at least this pilgrim's progress has a locus
and direction.

Langland's space is surrealistic. His opening places
the fair field full of folk, with clear allegorical meaning,
between tower and dungeon, Heaven and Hell. And
there may be a kind of allegorical logic in that no spatial relation, but only confusion, a heaping and piling
of images, follows in his picture of man's activities in
this wilderness earth. But artistic logic fades as one
scene reels and melts into the next, as characters—
sometimes whole troops of them—appear and dis-
appear or are forgotten. Dante, at every turn of the
road, can suddenly expose us to a shift of perspective,
a change of scale, without this surrealist feeling. In
Canto IV of the *Inferno,* in the midst of darkness, we
reach all of a sudden a seven-walled castle, and within
it a green field in a place "open, luminous, and high"
(v. 116), where the heroes of antiquity are visible. But
then we turn back with the narrator and guide to "the
part where there is nothing that shines" (151)—that is,
back to the spatial and locational frame that organizes
the whole. In *Piers Plowman* there is no going back.
The fair field and the mountain are transformed without notice into a great encampment—with ten thousand
tents for all the onlookers at the marriage of Meed.
We are suddenly present at the dickering over the marriage articles. Thence we go—by what road I know

not—to Westminster, before the King. In the next vision we have successively Conscience preaching to the people in the field and the confessions of the Seven Deadly Sins mentioned before; then in an unspecified locus, a thousand men throng together to seek St. Truth (Passus A V, 260); they walk or ride in many lands, bustling forth as beasts over valleys and hills. After a long journey they meet a pilgrim who says he has never heard of St. Truth. At that instant "Peter!" says a plowman, "I know him" (B V, 544), and from nowhere Piers Plowman materializes into the poem. He describes to them the road, by way of meekness and conscience and the ten commandments, to where truth resides in the human heart. The next spatial reference finds them all plowing Piers' half-acre. . . . And so the poem goes, existing in no one realm of space and location, invoking successive spatial images for limited and temporary effect without tending to the relations between them.

We can trace analogies of Langland's problematical structures, his unstable allegory and his emblematic realism, his surrealistic space, in other characteristics of his art. There is surely something of the same quality in his handling of the crucial but mysterious figure of Piers Plowman himself, who has been called the "supreme example of the poem's suggestive indefiniteness"[19]—with his various identities and sudden appearances and disappearances. There is something at once strange, difficult, and characteristic in a great many of Langland's transitions: abrupt, startling, sometimes so enigmatic that the sets of material that find themselves juxtaposed seem held together only by the force of the poet's personality. Bloomfield remarks that following some of the sequences of Langland's arguments and quotations "is like reading a commentary on an unknown text."[20] Yet another set of symptoms of the same basic character are those moments in the poem where, as a recent translator good-naturedly puts it, "it is not . . . clear who is speaking, whether the poet himself, the Dreamer, or one of the characters in the dream."[21]

In either explaining or at least sensing and responding to these problematic qualities of the poem, modern criticism has tended at times to turn away from the conventions and traditions of medieval thought and literature and to seek some solution in the peculiar condition of the poet himself. But one important appeal to tradition must still be noted: the poem's relation to the sermon. To put it briefly, and omitting all the well-known resemblances between the sermon and other genres we have mentioned, we are told that medieval sermon technique justified digression; digression was one of the best known procedures of rhetoric, and it is validated further by a religious purpose. If an opportunity for edification occurs, turning aside from the argument is morally justified; the spiritual purpose has precedence over the artistic. In this manner may be explained all manner of repetitions, sudden transitions, circuitous routings of thought, and apparently otiose amplifications, which we might otherwise attribute to carelessness or lack of art.[22]

Finding connections between *Piers Plowman* and sermon tradition is entirely justified—one could not imagine Langland in a world without sermons—but the connections apply better as to subject and to incidental traits of style than as to genre. The poem is manifestly not a sermon itself, and its depth and variety of "digressiveness" can hardly be matched in any known sermon. It is rather in its appeal to the question of "spiritual" purpose over "artistic" purpose that the argument from sermon-style has its force. And here I paraphrase from recent criticism of the poem: Sermon technique is utilitarian technique, the technique of the man who cares more for the spiritual significance of his words than for their art, less for narrative causality than for a higher order of truth; and we cannot doubt that Langland is such a man. Langland manifests some uncomfortableness at being a poet and writes in a very plain style for the alliterative tradition. The poem may not even be meant as art; for poetry in those days was a convenience, used for many utilitarian purposes as well. Thus Langland is interested as much in the spiritual background as in the narratives he commences, and a great deal of his background is at any rate not irrelevant to the story to which he periodically returns. His is an art of local tactics rather than of grand strategy; his coherence is thematic rather than narrative. A reformer and satirist, his mode is digressive and disintegrative, but his norms, at least, are consistent. End of paraphrase.[23]

A bolder development of this solution is also inherent in the poem's criticism. Here again I paraphrase: Writing the poem was a process of learning by the poet himself, thus the poem must always be in the process of revision and must always be unfinished. The perplexities of the poem are the exploratory perplexities of the poet's own mind, and they become those of the audience as well: it is the kaleidoscopic, problematical record of the search for Truth which Langland pursued all during his lifetime that *is* the poem. The poem is a record of cross-purposes, of repeated failures of inquiry, of the sometimes maddening slowness of the quest. We as readers are exposed to the same experience, undergo the same pains, enjoy the same exhilaration. End of paraphrase.[24]

This is an affecting argument, and there is much truth in it. It begins to explain how a work so bereft of the traditional apparatus of unity and coherence can have commanded so much attention and respect for so long. Though most of the critics I have paraphrased would still insist on the conscious art of the poem, the drift of the argument, as I have intimated, is to see the work not as art, but as a special sort of record of experience. It tends to see the audience as reliving that experience rather than as responding to art. By implication the author himself becomes the unifying feature of the work. The poem records the thoughts and feelings of a quite extraordinary man, passionate, moral, tender, humorous, dogged, and above all sincere. (The theories of a fictional Dreamer as unifying the poem simply melt in the felt heat of the poet's personality.) It is *his* earnestness and *his* plight that command our sympathy and retain our attention, even over the most difficult stretches of the work. *Piers Plowman* in this reading becomes, rather than a self-contained consciously wrought work of art, an intensely moving record of a man who wrote a lot of poetry in the midst of a prolonged spiritual struggle.

Whether we regard the problematic qualities of the poem's structure as arising from artistic failure, or from an artistic plan which we still only imperfectly understand, or as not properly belonging to art at all would seem to be partly, at least, a matter of attitude. For the critics agree remarkably on the describable qualities of the poem's structure, and in large part its artistic effect is independent of whether we think of it as proceeding from "art" or not. But as much as we should hesitate to find "defects" in a great monument of culture when the fault is likely to be in our own perception, it is difficult to stop looking at *Piers Plowman* as art. In the first place, to refuse to recognize what may be an artistic breakdown would be to refuse to listen to something fundamental about the artist and his epoch that the work is telling us. In the second place, quite simply, the poet was incontestably an artist. Even though that fact may not have dominated his intentions, his work raises the issue. The question of artistic structure is raised by great fragments of structural material disposed throughout the poem; the question of literary genre, by the unmistakable beginnings in it of half a dozen literary genres; the question of narrative art, by such famously successful episodes as the field full of folk (Prologue), the debate with the Doctor (Passus XIII), and the harrowing of Hell (Passus XVIII).

The issue is raised yet again, and settled, I think, when we consider the poem's poetic texture.[25] Here I shall review some of its most obvious stylistic traits in order to show that we are dealing with poet of great power, whose local style is of a piece with the structure of his poem.

The poet has an enormous range of tone—as great as Chaucer's. One extreme of it derives from his rich, easy capacity to render the familiar and concrete. I have already quoted one of the famous passages in which he creates a grotesque ugliness for satiric effect. He can use a version of this familiar style with penetrating sympathy as well:

The most needy aren oure neighebores, and we nyme good hede,

As prisones in puttes and poure folke in cotes,
Charged with children and chef lordes rente;
That thei with spynnynge may spare, spenen hit in
   hous-hyre.
Bothe in mylk and in mele to make with papelotes,
To a-glotye with here gurles that greden after fode.
Al-so hem-selue suffren muche hunger,
And wo in winter-tyme with wakynge a nyghtes
To ryse to the ruel to rocke the cradel,
Bothe to karde and to kembe, to clouten and to
   wasche,
To rubbe and to rely, russhes to pilie,
That reuthe is to rede othere in ryme shewe
The wo of these women that wonyeth in cotes. . . .

                                        [C X 71–83]

[The neediest people are our neighbors, if we pay some
attention, like the prisoners in dungeons and poor folk in
shacks, burdened with children and landlords' rent. Whatever they can save by spinning they spend for rent, and
for milk and meal to make porridge to fill up their children who cry for food. They themselves endure much
hunger, and pain in winter; they have to get up to rock
the cradle alongside the wall, to card and comb wool, to
mend and wash, to rub, and wind yarn, and peel rushes—
it is pitiful to read or tell in verse of the misery of these
women who live in shanties.]

The other extreme limit of his tone is supported by
perhaps his most notable gift as a poet: his capacity to
express the most elevated of religious feelings in the
simplest terms. He is one of the few medieval poets
besides Dante to have felt his way successfully back to
the "incarnational" style, the *sermo humilis* that reaches
sublimity of feeling without elaborate dependence on
the "high style" of rhetorical tradition.[26]

"And sith with thi self sone in owre sute deydest
On godefryday for mannes sake at ful tyme of the
    daye,
There thi-self ne thi sone no sorwe in deth feledest;
But in owre secte was the sorwe and thi sone it ladde,
    Captiuam duxit captiuitatem.
The sonne for sorwe ther-of les syȝte for a tyme
Aboute mydday whan most liȝte is and mele tyme of
    seintes;
Feddest with thi fresche blode owre forfadres in
    derknesse,
    Populus qui ambulabat in tenebris, vidit lucem
    magnam;
And thorw the liȝte that lepe oute of the Lucifer was
    blent,
And blewe alle thi blissed in-to the blissc of
    paradise."

                  [B V 495–503]

["And then, (God), with your own son clothed in our flesh you died on Good Friday for man's sake at high noon, and neither you nor your son felt the least pain in death. Rather the pain was in our flesh, and your son led it captive: 'he led captivity captive.' The sun (son) out of sorrow became blinded for a while, about midday, when there is the most light and it is the mealtime of saints; then you fed with your fresh blood our forefathers who were in darkness: 'The people who walked in darkness have seen a great light.' And through the light that leaped out of you Lucifer was blinded, and you blew all your blessed into the bliss of Paradise."]

The sequence describing the harrowing of Hell couples this sublime simplicity with flashes of the poet's dramatic powers:

Efte the liȝte bad vnlouke and Lucifer answered,
'What lorde artow?' quod Lucifer *'quis es iste?'*
'Rex glorie' the liȝte sone seide,
'And lorde of myȝte and of mayne and al manere
    vertues;
    dominus virtutum;
Dukes of this dym place anon undo this ȝates,
That Cryst may come in, the kinges sone of
    heuene.'

                           [B XVIII 313–318]

[Again the light commanded them to unlock, and Lucifer
answered, "What lord are you?" "Who is this man?" said
Lucifer. "The King of Glory," the light at once replied,
"and lord of might and power and of every goodness;
'The lord of virtues.' Dukes of this dark place, unlock
the gates at once, that Christ may come in, the son of the
King of Heaven."]

Christ's speech to Lucifer is perhaps the poetic high-
point of the poem:

    'For I, that am lorde of lyf, loue is my drynke,
And for that drynke to-day I deyde vpon erthe.
I fauȝte so, me threstes ȝet for mannes soule sake;
May no drynke me moiste ne my thruste slake,
Tyl the vendage falle in the vale of Iosephath,
That I drynke riȝte ripe must *resureccio mortuorum*,
And thanne shal I come as a kynge crouned with
    angeles,
And han out of helle alle mennes soules.'

                           [B XVIII 363–370]

["For I, the Lord of Life, drink only love, and for that
drink today I died on earth. I fought so, that I am thirsty
yet for man's soul's sake. No drink can refresh me nor
slake my thirst till vintage-time comes in the valley of

Jehoshaphat, and I drink the fresh new wine of the resurrection of the dead. Then shall I come as a King, crowned with angels, and fetch out of hell all men's souls."]

The poet's work is marked by another rare quality, his gift for the arresting image, that supports effects ranging from incongruity and surprise to the profoundest metaphorical illumination of the subject. I can quote only a few of the examples familiar to every reader. Langland congenitally disliked lawyers:

Thow my3test better mete the myste on Maluerne hulles,
Than gete a momme of here mouthe but money were shewed.

[B Prol. 214–215]

[You could sooner measure the mist on the Malvern Hills than get a word out of their mouths before showing your money.]

and timeservers:

. . . ful proude-herted men pacient of tonge,
And boxome as of berynge to burgeys and to lordes,
And to pore peple han peper in the nose. . . .

[B XV 195–197]

[. . . very proud men who are humble in speech, submissive in their conduct toward important citizens and noblemen, but to the poor (as snobbish) as if they had pepper in their noses.]

and the rich:

Clerkes and kni3tes welcometh kynges ministrales,
And for loue of the lorde litheth hem at festes;

Muche more, me thenketh, riche men schulde
Haue beggeres byfore hem, the whiche ben goddes
    ministrales,
. . .
For-thi I rede ȝow riche, reueles whan ȝe maketh,
For to solace ȝoure soules suche ministrales to haue;
The pore, for a fol sage syttynge at the heyȝ table,
And a lered man, to lere the what oure lorde suffred,
For to saue thi soule fram Sathan thin enemy,
And fithel the, with-out flaterynge, of gode Friday the
    storye. . . .

[B XIII 437–440, 442–447]

[Clerks and knights welcome the king's minstrels, and out
of respect for their master they listen to them at feasts.
There is more reason, I think, for rich men to have at
table beggars, who are God's minstrels. . . . So I advise
you rich men to have minstrels like these to care for your
souls when you make your revels—the poor rather than
a wise fool sitting at the high table, and a learned man
to teach you what our lord suffered to save your soul
from Satan, your enemy, and to fiddle you without flat-
tery the story of Good Friday.]

Defective clerics brought out some of his most striking
imagery:

Thus thei dryuele at her deyse the deite to knowe,
And gnawen god with the gorge whan her gutte is fulle.

[B X 56–57]

[Thus they drivel at the high table as if they knew the
Deity, and when their guts are full find God in their
gullets.]

'I shal Iangle to this Iurdan with his Iust wombe. . . .'[27]

[B XIII 83]

["I shall dispute with this pot-bellied jordan. . . ."]

I rede eche a blynde bosarde do bote to hym-selue. . . .
                                        [B X 266]

> [I advise each of these blind buzzards to look after
> himself. . . .]

In passages dealing with ordinary matters of faith and
doctrine, the apparent ingenuousness of the imagery is
sometimes highly arresting. Thus God "may do with
the day-sterre what hym deore lyketh" (A VI 83),
"Adam and Eue eten apples vnrosted" (B V 612),
and Soul is described as "a sotyl thinge with-al, one
with-outen tonge and teeth" (B XV 12–13). Regarding the salvation of the poor,

> . . . none sonner saued ne sadder of bileue,
> Than plowmen and pastoures and pore comune
>   laboreres,
> Souteris and shepherdes; suche lewide Iottis
> Percen with a *pater-noster* the paleis of heuene. . . .
>   [B X 458–461]

> [. . . none are more likely to be saved nor steadier in
> their faith than plowmen and herdsmen and poor com-
> mon laborers, cobblers and shepherds; such ignorant
> nobodies can pierce the palace of heaven with the Lord's
> Prayer . . .]

On wasting words, the poet writes:

> Lesynge of tyme, treuthe wote the sothe!
> Is moste yhated vp erthe of hem that beth in heuene,
> And sitthe to spille speche, that spyre is of grace,
> And goddes gleman and a game of heuene;
> Wolde neuere the faithful fader his fithel were
>   vntempred,
> Ne his gleman a gedelynge, a goer to tauernes!
>   [B IX 98–103]

[Wasting of time, God knows, is the thing on earth most
hated by those in heaven, and next is wasting of speech,
that is the sprout of grace and God's minstrel and a pas-
time of heaven; the faithful Father never meant his fiddle
to be untuned, nor his minstrel to be a scoundrel, a goer
to taverns!]

The indispensable nature of charity brings out two
memorable similes in half a dozen lines:

For thouʒ ʒe be trewe of ʒowre tonge and trewliche
    wynne,
And as chaste as a childe that in cherche wepeth,
But if ʒe louen lelliche and lene the poure,
Such good as god ʒow sent godelich parteth,
ðe ne haue na more meryte in masse ne in houres
Than Malkyn of hire maydenhode that no man desireth.
                                                [B I 177–182]

[For though you be true of tongue, and earn your living
honestly, and be as innocent as a child that weeps in
church, unless you are sincerely charitable, and give to
the poor, properly sharing the goods that God has sent
you, you will get no more credit from attending masses
and services than Molly from her maidenhead that
nobody wants.]

The Trinity of course evoked the poet's powers of
analogy. During a complex comparison between the
Trinity and a torch, he takes up the gift of the Holy
Ghost:

And as glowande gledes gladieth nouʒte this
    werkmen,
That worchen and waken in wyntres niʒtes,
As doth a kex or a candel that cauʒte hath fyre and
    blaseth,
Namore doth sire ne sone ne seynt spirit togyderes,

Graunteth no grace ne forȝifnesse of synnes,
Til the holi goste gynne to glowe and to blase.
[B XVII 217–222]

[And just as glowing coals do not cheer those workmen who stay up and work on winter nights as much as does a torch or a candle that has been lit and burns with a flame, so neither the Father, nor the Son, nor the Holy Spirit together will grant anyone grace or forgiveness of sins until the Holy Ghost begins to burn and to blaze.]

The most striking imagery in the poem comes perhaps in Passus I, in reference to the Incarnation:

For trewthe telleth that loue is triacle of heuene;
May no synne be on him sene that vseth that spise,
And alle his werkes he wrouȝte with loue as him
        liste;
. . .
    For heuen myȝte nouȝte holden it, it was so heuy
        of hym-self,
Tyl it hadde of the erthe yeten his fylle;
    And whan it haued of this folde flesshe and
            blode taken,
Was neuere leef vpon lynde liȝter ther-after,
And portatyf and persant as the poynt of a nedle,
That myȝte non armure it lette ne none heiȝ walles.
[B I 146–148, 151–156]

[For it is God's truth that love is the sovereign medicine of heaven; there is not a sin to be seen on him who uses that kind. And God made all his works with love, as it pleased him; . . . For heaven could not hold it, it was so heavy in itself, until it had eaten its fill of this earth. And after it had taken on flesh and blood of this world, there was never a leaf on a linden tree more light; it was as delicate and piercing as the point of a needle. No armor or high walls could keep it out.]

There is another dominant trait of his style that is
related to the surprise effect of his imagery: the line
or half line that suddenly turns the mood or thought
around, often with a satiric snap:

Pilgrymes and palmers pliȝted hem togidere
To seke seynt Iames and seyntes in Rome.
Thei went forth in here wey with many wise tales,
And hadden leue to lye al here lyf after.

[B Prol. 46–49]

[Pilgrims and palmers joined together to visit the shrines
of St. James in Compostela and of the saints in Rome.
They made their way there with a lot of smart talk and
felt free to tell lies about it for the rest of their lives.]

Persones and parisch prestes pleyned hem to the
    bischop,
That here parisshes were pore sith the pestilence
    tyme,
To haue a lycence and a leue at London to dwelle,
And syngen there for symonye, for siluer is swete.

[B Prol. 83–86]

[Parsons and parish priests complained to the bishop that
their parishes had been poverty-stricken since the time
of the plague—just to get permission to live in London
and sing masses there for profit, for silver is sweet.]

And that is the professioun appertly that appendeth
    for knyȝtes,
And nouȝt to fasten a Fryday in fyue score
    wynter. . . .

[B I 98–99]

[And that is obviously the proper activity for knights, and
not to fast one Friday in a hundred winters. . . .]

Langland has no inhibitions about colloquial language.
Here Learning describes a Chaucerian monk:

> A priker on a palfray fro manere to manere,
> An heep of houndes at his ers as he a lorde were.
>   [B X 308–309]

> [A galloper on horseback from manor to manor, with a
> bunch of dogs at his ass as if he were a lord.]

Learning's cousin, Lady Study, feels strongly about
intellectual pretentiousness:

> Wilneth neuere to wite whi that god wolde
> Suffre Sathan his sede to bigyle,
> Ac bileue lelly in the lore of holicherche,
> And preye hym of pardoun and penaunce in thi lyue,
> And for his moche mercye to amende ȝow here.
> For alle that wilneth to wyte the weyes of god almiȝty,
> I wolde his eye were in his ers and his fynger after. . . .
>   [B X 117–123]

> [Never try to find out why God would let Satan deceive
> his children, but believe faithfully in the teaching of
> Holy Church, and pray God for pardon, and to let you do
> penance while you are alive, and out of his great mercy
> to correct you on earth. As for anyone who wants to pry
> into the ways of God almighty, I wish his eye were up
> his ass and his finger after it. . . .]

Langland's poetic rhythms would be at best difficult
to deal with, and in small compass I cannot attempt it.
But I must advert in passing to a rhythmical trait that
seems to be characteristic of his work both in large
and small: its continual susceptibility to irruptions—
whether in the poetic line or in the narrative. Some of
the poetic texture—the metaphorical or referential sur-

prise described above—contributes to this rhythm. In addition the reader soon learns to recognize as part of Langland's style the sharp transitions between scenes and the sudden appearances of characters, sometimes with interjectional force:

'Peter!' quod a plowman and put forth his hed. . . .
[B V 544]

'ȝee! baw for bokes!' quod one was broken out of helle,
Hiȝte *Troianus*. . . .
[B XI 135–136]

["Yeah! Bah for books!" said a man named Trajan, just broken out of hell. . . .]

'ȝe, bawe!' quod a brewere, 'I wil nouȝt be reuled. . . .'
[B XIX 394]

Rhythmically of a piece are the occasional dramatic irruptions of "pure tene," sheer anger. Those of Piers the Plowman himself seem to set an exemplary tone of divine impatience for the poem as a whole:

'Now, bi the peril of my soule!' quod Pieres al in pure tene. . . .
[B VI 119]

And Pieres for pure tene pulled it atweyne. . . .
[B VII 116]

(thus suddenly setting off the most difficult of the poem's puzzles);

And Pieres for pure tene that o pile he lauȝte,
And hitte after hym, happe how it myȝte. . . .
[B XVI 86–87]

[And Piers in sheer anger seized one of the staffs and
swung at him, whatever might happen. . . .]

There are yet other sources of periodic and often
unpredicted interruptions of the poem's rhythms: the
shifts of focus from individual to scene, well described
by John Lawlor; the frequent changes of the narrative's
apparent pace—what Rosemary Woolf has termed "an
alternate dawdling and darting movement;"[28] the actual suspensions of the narrative with direct address by
the narrator to the audience; and doubtless others yet
to be identified. While the poem contains many com-
fortingly repeated motifs,[29] and great stretches of relatively stable didactic utterance—enough for Morton
Bloomfield to have found in its tone and diction a
source of what "stability" it has[30]—we still come away
from it with something of the feeling that in it anything might have happened.

The artistic character of *Piers Plowman,* when it is
viewed as a whole as we are attempting to view it now,
has a strange integrity and coherence. Many of the formal and stylistic traits we have observed can be found
in other respectable medieval poems. I venture to say
that no other work of the Middle Ages has them all.
Together they are quite distinctive, but they are also
peculiarly harmonious. Even the poem's seemingly
most disparate traits have a common basis. It is not
only that "there is a consistency in the very lack of
consistency," as Talbot Donaldson has remarked of
the art of the C-reviser;[31] the poet does not seem to
have been aware of inconsistency as a problem. Thus
the ease with which the poem can at one moment
evoke simultaneously the realistic and the sublime
seems to issue from the same mentality, the same sensi-

bility, that produces the violent transitions and the equivalences that seem startling. It is as if the poet felt none of his disjunctures as such because to him the concrete and the abstract, the actual and the moral had themselves taken on a special sort of equivalence. I say a special sort, because the capacity to see the spiritual in the concrete and to aver the reality of the spiritual and moral realms were hallmarks of medieval mentality in general. In *Piers*, however, they are not only equivalent, but mingled; the borders and distinctions have melted or collapsed.[32] This, as it seems to me, is the import of the artistic character of the poem. The obscurity of the larger plan, the seemingly capricious interplay of debate, pilgrimage, and quest, and of mimetics and didacticism; the periodic establishment and collapse of the dream-frame; the shiftiness of space; the paradox of graphic power and pictorial diffuseness;[33] the alternations within a great range of tone and temper; the shiftiness of rhythm—all these produce a curiously homogeneous artistic effect that for lack of a better term I have called surrealistic.

The art of *Piers Plowman* is assuredly the creation of a quite remarkable personality, but it is also a response to a cultural situation. Viewed in this way, the form and style of the poem seem to be saying something more than do its overt arguments. In the sequence of his arguments, Langland seems to me finally to lead us, on some level, toward the Truth he sought. The uncontroverted advice of Holy Church, the consistent recommendation of natural wisdom, and the triumphant vision of the Passion and the harrowing of Hell are the most obvious controlling points of the poem's motion; and there is an aura of a new understanding, if not a final resolution, in the closing scenes which, drawn from life in fourteenth-century England, suggestively parallel the opening scenes of the poem. But nevertheless, the more that criticism reveals the manifold, intricate filiations between the thought of the poem and orthodox medieval doctrine, and the closer we are brought to sensing the intended directions of its argument,[34] the more the form and style of the poem seem to envelop it in a sort of pathos. For if the thought of the poem is orthodox, Christian, and hopeful, its art suggests instability: the imminent collapse of orthodoxy and failure of hope. The great artistic schemes that Langland attempts and abandons had all been adapted before him to expressing the security of the medieval Christian vision. His failure with them, his failure to organize and "see" by means of them, suggests that for a man of his sensitivity, responding to the culture around him, those schemes had lost their meaning. For him, the road to the New Jerusalem has become newly devious, the structure of the moral world newly problematical. His passionate criticisms, his earnest exhortations, seem all the more urgent for issuing from within this strange, surrealistic structure. The range and texture of his style have the same ring: urgent, sincere, and somehow pathetic, as if marshalled desperately against some unavoidable crisis. The poem has been well called "the epic of the dying Middle Ages,"[35] but it carries the instability of the epoch in its very structure and style as well as in its argument.

If we are to see a cultural significance in the art of *Piers Plowman,* we should be able to compare it with the art of some of his contemporaries. It would be particularly comforting to find, for instance, a well-developed tradition of "surrealism" in late medieval England. Unfortunately, the analogies to Langland's art that I have so far been able to trace are rather far afield. There is assuredly something surrealistic in late-medieval pictorial art; we see it everywhere in the margins of manuscripts, and I am not the first whom Langland's style has reminded of that of Hieronymus Bosch.[36] Closer to Langland in time is a group of Tuscan painters in the generation after the Black Death, in an atmosphere of guilt and fear, whose style can be described in terms that are like those I have used to describe *Piers Plowman.* They turn from the current of realism stemming from Giotto, to a style more rigid, formalistic, pious, and mystical. They reject perspective and are full of paradox, particularly in the sense of space. A St. Matthew by Orcagna is described by the art historian Millard Meiss as exhibiting a tension incapable of resolution, "Arising as it does from an interpenetration of the natural and unnatural, the physical and the abstract." Meiss suggests that this quality of the painting reflects a polarization in the society between strenuous religiosity on the one hand and moral and religious dissidence on the other.[37]

Though Langland is also a post-Plague artist—he continually insists on the moral import of pestilence—important parallels to the corresponding quality of his style are not obvious in England, whether in painting or in literature. The strongest resemblance is to be found in Chaucer's *House of Fame,* but that work is by far Chaucer's most puzzling one. Even the complex, ironic structuring of so variegated a satire as the *Nun's Priest's Tale* produces a sense of assurance and security quite foreign to *Piers Plowman.*

If we lack satisfying contemporary analogues to the art of *Piers Plowman,* we can still learn something by contrast. *Pearl* and *Sir Gawain* are also searches for salvation and for perfection, and are also conducted by a man who was at once a moralist and artist. The distance between them is instructive. It is almost the extreme range in form and style that contemporaneous works of art, in the same stream of history, could be imagined to produce. On the one hand an almost obsessive unity, an overpowering devotion to artifice, as if the work of art were in itself an assertion of the truths it was testing, and the creation of the work, not a denial of crisis, but at most expressing it obliquely and at a remove. On the other hand, a direct facing, an immersion in the problematic character of the times, to the point where the poem with the poet, having together been submitted to the crisis itself, seem to have become in part its victims.

IV

CHAUCER: IRONY AND ITS ALTERNATIVES

IT IS PERHAPS NO COINCIDENCE THAT LANGLAND'S *Piers Plowman* reached its full scope in the same decade as Chaucer's *House of Fame*. The *House of Fame* is Chaucer's most flamboyant and puzzling work, also an unconventional dream-allegory, capricious, varied to extremes, shifting in tone and structure, strung out between serious formality and comic realism. If these works show both poets confronting the same cultural situation with a similar variety of formal and stylistic resources, Chaucer's later career shows that he came to a different and more peaceful conclusion. In the *Canterbury Tales* he uses the pilgrimage form to enclose and control a wide range of experience. The variety of texture in the *Tales* and in the *Troilus*—a matter of exquisitely adjusted and contrasting patches of value —is a source of irony, a controlled irony. And in our perspective, at least, it is irony, comic or grave, that is Chaucer's characteristic response to the fourteenth-century dilemma.[1] His irony, if it does not resolve the contradictions and disparities of late-medieval life, embraces, displays, enjoys, makes capital of them. The great virtues that Chaucer teaches are perception and tolerance. The disparity between what men might be and what they are fascinated the *Pearl* poet as well, and also produced a certain irony in his works. But he is not nearly so tolerant or liberal as Chaucer, for whom ironic appreciation of what life has to offer is almost a norm. Langland, too, is a respectable ironist, but even less ultimately one. Langland is equipped with a sense of the facts of life equal to Chaucer's, but with a moral idealism so urgent and so powerful that it continually threatens to yank irony, or any other complex or tentative view, out of the question.

Chaucer's irony must impress us with its depth and congeniality. It is not only a literary and structural device, but a personal propensity. There is in Chaucer's basic habits of discourse already a mixture of relaxation and intensity, naturalness and artifice, familiarity and distance, colloquialism and learned sophistication—a mixture ready at any moment to explode with ironic effect. His development as a poet may be viewed, in fact, as a progressive discovery and exploitation of this propensity.[2]

It would be safe, therefore, to imagine that the mature Chaucer, the Chaucer of *Canterbury Tales* Fragment A (the *General Prologue,* the Knight's, Miller's, Reeve's and Cook's tales) for instance, actually came to feel this as his very own mode, if not consciously, then by instinct and experience. For the scheme of the *Canterbury Tales* could not be improved upon, with its built-in sequence of tales, not only to create a structural irony in the juxtaposition of the tales to be written, but, once it had accommodated some of the older things already in Chaucer's desk, to confer on those, too, an ironic character with which they had not originally been invested. The structure of the *Tales,* then, actually masks the observation, readily apparent in the *House of Fame,* that Chaucer was not always an ironist, was sometimes not at all in that mood, and may for a long time not even have felt irony to be his "solution."

The Chaucer of the *Retractation,* perhaps facing his death, undoubtedly felt himself to be, if not first then last, a Christian, and there is an unwaveringly orthodox profession of faith in other of Chaucer's endings—as of his *Troilus* and his *Nun's Priest's Tale.* The logic of his ironic structure, pushed toward a consideration of ends, ultimate realities, provided in fact a justification of orthodox faith. Serious irony can be made finally to expose the instability of this brittle world and by implication to turn our attention to a stable world of faith in God. Chaucer was always a Christian, then, and that solution for Chaucer lay beyond irony. The faith of the *Retractation,* of the *Troilus* Epilogue, of even the *Nun's Priest's Tale,* is a grand and final thing, and it is validated by the rich experience that has gone into the ironic vision even as the latter is finally transcended. This, then, I should call not so much a working alternative to irony as a final consequence of it.

I am laboring here to mark out this source, this location, this kind of religiosity for a number of reasons. First, to anticipate the reader's natural objections to my suggesting that irony was close to being Chaucer's ultimate position. Second, to make clear that I do not read any of Chaucer's secular works as covert religious allegories. Third, to distinguish this solemn, ultimate religiosity—perhaps we might call it eschatological faith—from a different current of religious feeling in Chaucer's works: that is, the religiosity around which are clustered feelings of tenderness and pathos, and which is often associated with motherhood, little children, and the cult of the Virgin Mary. If we take Chaucer's *ABC* to be an early work, as it may well be, we can see that this current of religious feeling must have been for quite a long time for Chaucer a major alternative to irony. The character and implications of this whole vein in Chaucer's work will occupy a good deal of our attention in this chapter. But before we turn to them, we must first make a survey of some other of Chaucer's alternatives.

Even had we no *House of Fame,* a line drawn from the *Book of the Duchess* through the *Parliament of Fowls* would have shown the growth of Chaucer's famous comic realism. Chaucer was capable of solemnity, but even on the solemn occasion of elegizing the Duchess of Lancaster we sense a certain restiveness in him. He cannot quite abide the idea of elegy pure and simple, and out comes the characterization of the narrator with its unmistakably Chaucerian touches of humor and naive realism. There is no victim of irony but the narrator himself, and he remains subordinate, serving only to heighten, not to complicate or qualify, the elegiac feeling; but he is there. In the *Parliament of Fowls* the lesser fowls take up the style of his strain of realism and connect it with a set of attitudes, a position. But by now the position is already safely embraced in a larger plan, and we recognize in the *Parliament*'s ironic balance between realism and idealism in love a perfect foretaste of Chaucer's classic stance.

The dramatic realism in the *House of Fame,* by which I mean Chaucer's characterization of the loquacious and pedantic Eagle, is not similarly held firm in an ironic balance with something else. It floats almost free, almost an end in itself. With its technical brilliance, which conveys a palpable joy in the characterization, it suggests strongly that at one moment Chaucer might have given himself up to the dramatic-realistic mode and finally to the implications of attitude that would inevitably follow from it. Indeed, a couple of times he may have come close. Pandarus, by the Third Book of the *Troilus,* has grown alarmingly vivid, alarmingly sympathetic, alarmingly real. Many a reader, I am sure, has already noticed the amount of Chaucer in him—Chaucer the court official and man of affairs, intimate of nobility, skillful, reliable, well-read, tactful agent and messenger, who knows the "olde daunce" (his sister-in-law, after all, is mistress of the greatest Duke of the realm). But no—Chaucer is also an idealist and moralist, and Pandarus is finally held firm in the larger perspective created by Troilus and by the poem's denouement.

Barely held firm, but held firm nevertheless, is also the Wife of Bath. We do not come away from a reading of her *Prologue* converted sensualists; that is proof enough of Chaucer's firm grip. But I am not certain I understand how he does it. It is not simply by impregnating the *Prologue* with ill-veiled examples of her gross misunderstanding of Scripture.[3] No one would expect her to have a theologian's understanding of Scripture. She wins the contests described in her *Prologue;* for the moment, at least, wins Chaucer; wins us (or many of us); wins the contest offered by the Clerk —that skinny scholar could never turn the world from sin; and if you look not far about you, now that love is no longer sin, you will see that she has won the contest with history. Yet Chaucer finally holds her in perspective; not solely with any a priori moral doctrine, nor with any single counterbalancing character or tale, but perhaps with the cumulative wisdom of all of them. "I have had my world as in my tyme" is a compelling motto; but Chaucer feels, and makes us feel, ultimately, that it is not enough. If anything, it lacks irony.

There is yet another serious brush that Chaucer has
with the implications of dramatic realism, serious not
in extent, but in depth. I refer to the bottomless pool
we may be looking into toward the end of the *Pardoner's Tale*. The Pardoner is, like Pandarus, something akin to Chaucer himself, in this case akin as
rhetorician and storyteller. He is the most accomplished
literary artist among Chaucer's characters. It is interesting to speculate whether there is any connection
between the almost grotesque perversity of his description—he is the most "unnatural" of the Canterbury
pilgrims—and some special baseness Chaucer may feel
in the perversion of his talent. At the end of the tale
there does seem to be an odd and special contact between Chaucer and his Pardoner. As a good many
people read it, the Pardoner's demonstration sermon
ends with a last blast of rhetorical fireworks, followed
by a sales pitch to his imagined demonstration audience, followed by a brief explanatory address to his
new friends the Canterbury pilgrims. This brief address, beginning "And lo, sires, thus I preche," has an
exquisite human interest, for in it the practised and
hardened confidence man for once puts by his cynicism—warmed perhaps by friendship and ale—and
invokes, not his own pardon for his companions, but
Christ's, "for that is best." Let me quote the passage:

> "O cursed synne of alle cursednesse!
> O traytours homycide, O wikkednesse!
> O glotonye, luxurie, and hasardrye!
> Thou blasphemour of Crist with vileynye
> And othes grete, of usage and of pride!
> Allas! mankynde, how may it bitide
> That to thy creatour, which that the wroghte,

And with his precious herte-blood thee boghte,
Thou art so fals and so unkynde, allas?
    Now, goode men, God foryeve yow youre trespas,
And ware yow fro the synne of avarice!
Myn hooly pardoun may yow alle warice,
So that ye offre nobles or sterlynges,
Or elles silver broches, spoones, rynges.
Boweth youre heed under this hooly bulle!
Cometh up, ye wyves, offreth of youre wolle!
Youre names I entre heer in my rolle anon;
Into the blisse of hevene shul ye gon.
I yow assoille, by myn heigh power,
Yow that wol offre, as clene and eek as cleer
As ye were born.—And lo, sires, thus I preche.
And Jhesu Crist, that is oure soules leche,
So graunte yow his pardoun to receyve,
For that is best; I wol yow nat deceyve."

                                [895–918]

Not one of the pilgrims responds. Rather, the Pardoner begins again, with a crude and cynical sales pitch addressed directly to them: "But, sires, oo thyng forgat I in my tale. . . ."

At this point variant interpretations are possible. We need stage directions and there are none. Why does the Pardoner so abruptly change his tack? Is he serious, or patently joking? Reading the analogous passage in the *Roman de la Rose*—where the character Faus-Semblant admits to his hearers at the end of his confession that despite his present candor he would trick them if he could[4]—I am led to think that the Pardoner is meant to be serious. If he is, the sequence of candor, of honest piety, and then of redoubled cynicism in this reading is almost terrifying in its moral range. Harry

Bailly thinks he is serious, and replies with obscene directness. But either way, the Canterbury pilgrims must be imagined to have been left thunderstruck by the sermon, as affected as any of the Pardoner's provincial audiences. It is a moment of extraordinary psychological complexity; and with Harry Bailly's response to the Pardoner we are for a moment absorbed in the interest of the Pardoner's personality. Chaucer's crucial leaving-out of the stage directions here makes everything depend on the sheer dramatics of the reading; it is a moment almost unique in his works. Behind it we glimpse, possibly, a man like the Pardoner possessed by pride in his own technique, but both he and the Pardoner pass from sight at the next moment. Chaucer may have flirted with, but was never captured by, an absorption with either human personality or artistic technique.

Turning to yet another of Chaucer's alternatives to irony, we can see clearly that French courtly idealism, with the rather fragile poetry it generated, could not become a major solution for Chaucer any more than could realism. Like realism it early and importantly enters into, and its ideals are qualified by, the ironic configuration. Yet for a considerable while Chaucer seems nevertheless to have felt the pull of an unqualified secular idealism. The composition and revision of the *Legend of Good Women* in the late 1380s and '90s, after the fully ironic position of the *Troilus* had been achieved, must be a symptom of a periodic resurgence of a mood of idealism that is otherwise registered in the *Anelida and Arcite,* the *Knight's Tale* and the *Franklin's Tale.* The *Anelida* and the *Knight's Tale,* along with some framing passages of the *Troilus,* show Chaucer furthermore experimenting with a heroic style.

In this, Chaucer seems to be attempting to overcome a certain deficiency of expressiveness in the French courtly tradition while adhering to the chivalric and erotic ideals it represents. He is reaching back, as did in some sense every generation of English poets after him for centuries, reaching back to the heroic classics —in this case Vergil and Statius—and like some later generations, coming up not so much with the classics as with the Italians.

The epic-sublime style of Vergil was for a long time beyond the art of the Middle Ages except in such direct imitations as Joseph of Exeter's *De Bello Troiano.*[5] It is curious that the vernacular French courtly tradition represented by the *Book of the Duchess,* by Deschamps, Machaut, Froissart as poet, Guillaume de Lorris, and even Chrétien de Troyes, almost totally lacks the epic and heroic note. Chaucer heard echoes of Anglo-Saxon epic style in some second- and third-rate English romances of his own times; and early French romance, in the decades when it is still not certain of itself, not certain whether it is romance or epic, has a martial note related to that of the *chanson de geste.* But as soon as the connection between chivalry and courtly love is firmly made, the iron goes out of medieval narrative style, no matter how many hand-to-hand combats remain. The recapturing of "classical" epic style in the vernacular before Milton is largely the work of the Italians of the Middle Ages and early Renaissance— from Dante and Boccaccio through Ariosto and Tasso —and to this labor Chaucer seems to have lent himself for perhaps a decade in the 1370s and '80s.

The role of the Italians in guiding Chaucer's stylistic experiment was long ago noted by Root:

From Italy, and primarily I think from Dante, came the inspiration to tell the story of Troilus in the *bel stilo alto*; to write in the vernacular with the dignity and elevation which mark the great ancients. . . . Similar in character to his debt to Dante is Chaucer's debt to the *Teseide* of Boccaccio, a poem in its style as ornate and elevated as the *Filostrato* is simple and direct.[6]

The *Teseida,* full of reminiscences of the *Divine Comedy,* the *Aeneid,* and *Thebaid,* was in fact quite self-consciously designed to revive the epic style. Boccaccio announces in its final stanzas that virtue and love, two of the three great poetic subjects (defined by Dante in the *De Vulgari eloquentia*), have already been treated by vernacular poets "con bello stilo"; and he makes invocation to his own book, which will be first to sing of the third subject, arms:

> ma tu, o libro, primo a lor cantare
> di Marte fai gli affanni sostenuti,
> nel volgar lazio piú mai non veduti.[7]

[But you, my book, will be the first to sing to them of the painful labors undergone in war, hitherto unheard of in the vulgar tongue.]

As Root suggests, Chaucer clearly felt the pull of the classical-sublime in Dante's style; and as a close reader of the *Teseida* he was surely aware of Boccaccio's stylistic program as well. But if the *House of Fame* is any indication (and if we have the sequence of his works here correctly), Chaucer's earliest contact with the Italians did not at once suggest that they could teach him how to do epic style in the vernacular. As with almost all the other sources or inspirations behind the *House of Fame,* Chaucer here seems stimulated by the Italians without being directed by them. The long summary of the *Aeneid* in *House of Fame,* Book I, does not in the slightest suggest epic style. Chaucer rather, with the lion's share of the summary given to the Dido episode, falls back toward the French and Ovidian mode, the mode of pathetic female complaint, pointing along the axis of the *Legend of Good Women* and Dorigen at the seashore. Chaucer does make epic invocation to Cipris and the muses at the opening of Book II, in a passage mingling reminiscences of Dante and Boccaccio, but precedes it with a handful of verses so un-epic that the passage must be heard to be believed:

> Now herkeneth, every maner man
> That Englissh understonde kan,
> And listeneth of my drem to lere.
> For now at erste shul ye here
> So sely an avisyon,
> That Isaye, ne Scipion,
> Ne kyng Nabugodonosor,
> Pharoo, Turnus, ne Elcanor,
> Ne mette such a drem as this!
> Now faire blisfull, O Cipris,
> So be my favour at this tyme!
> And ye, me to endite and ryme
> Helpeth, that on Parnaso duelle,
> Be Elicon, the clere welle.
> O Thought, that wrot al that I mette,
> And in the tresorye hyt shette
> Of my brayn, now shal men se

Yf any vertu in the be,
To tellen al my drem aryght.
Now kythe thyn engyn and myght!

[509–528]

Chaucer does connect the Italians and an epic style in the unfinished *Anelida and Arcite;* apparently he had both the *Teseida* and the *Thebaid* before him as he wrote the first seventy lines. The remainder of the poem, except for its complex metrical form, could well have been included in the *Legend of Good Women,* where it would have ranked among the less interesting pieces in that rather bland collection. But the opening of the *Anelida* is important and fascinating, being Chaucer's first sustained passage in the epic mode. It is full of his sense of its importance, with its multiple invocations, its citations of antiquity and authority, and then its beginning of the narrative in the highest of the high style. Every student of Chaucer's art should ponder the comparison between the quite respectable martial poetry of his description of Duke Theseus here with its later perfection in the *Knight's Tale.* I quote only a few lines of each; here *Anelida:*

Beforn this duk, in signë of victorie,
The trompes come, and in his baner large
The ymage of Mars; and, in token of glorie,
Men myghte sen of tresour many a charge,
Many a bright helm, and many a spere and targe,
Many a fresh knyght, and many a blysful route,
On hors, on fote, in al the feld aboute.

[29–35]

And here the *Knight's Tale:*

> The rede statue of Mars, with spere and targe,
> So shyneth in his white baner large,
> That alle the feeldes glyteren up and doun;
> And by his baner born is his penoun
> Of gold ful riche, in which ther was ybete
> The Mynotaur, which that he slough in Crete.
> Thus rit this duc, thus rit this conquerour,
> And in his hoost of chivalrie the flour. . . .
>
> [975–982]

The epic mode in *Anelida,* from what we can tell, remains decoration; Chaucer does not yet suggest a reconnection of love and heroism. But he is already using the mode as a kind of framing device, as he does in the *Troilus* and the *Knight's Tale.* In the *Troilus* the passages of epic style have a number of functions; one is to connect Troilus' valor in war with his worthiness for love. Here is the heroic Troilus seen by Criseyde:

> This Troilus sat on his baye steede,
> Al armed, save his hed, ful richely;
> And wownded was his hors, and gan to blede,
> On which he rood a pas ful softely.
> But swich a knyghtly sighte, trewely,
> As was on hym, was nought, withouten faille,
> To loke on Mars, that god is of bataille.
>
> So lik a man of armes and a knyght
> He was to seen, fulfilled of heigh prowesse;
> For bothe he hadde a body and a myght
> To don that thing, as wel as hardynesse;
> And ek to seen hym in his gere hym dresse,
> So fressh, so yong, so weldy seemed he,

It was an heven upon hym for to see.

His helm tohewen was in twenty places,
That by a tyssew heng his bak byhynde;
His sheeld todasshed was with swerdes and maces,
In which men myght many an arwe fynde
That thirled hadde horn and nerf and rynde;
And ay the peple cryde, "Here cometh oure joye,
And, next his brother, holder up of Troye!"
                                              [II, 624–644]

But the heroic Troilus is ironically exposed to the perspective of Pandarus' realism. Here is the same hero as
seen by his friend:

This Pandarus com lepyng in atones,
And seyde thus, "Who hath ben wel ibete
To-day with swerdes and with slynge-stones,
But Troilus, that hath caught hym an hete?"
An gan to jape, and seyde, "Lord, so ye swete!"
                                              [II, 939–943]

Elsewhere the epic style helps to link the fate of the
lovers with the fate of Troy:

Yt is wel wist how that the Grekes, stronge
In armes, with a thousand shippes, wente
To Troiewardes, and the cite longe
Assegeden, neigh ten yer or they stente,
And in diverse wise and oon entente,
The ravysshyng to wreken of Eleyne,
By Paris don, they wroughten all hir peyne.
                                              [I, 57–63]

Liggyng in oost, as I have seyd er this,
The Grekys stronge aboute Troie town,
Byfel that, whan that Phebus shynyng is

Upon the brest of Hercules lyoun,
That Ector, with ful many a bold baroun,
Caste on a day with Grekes for to fighte,
As he wont, to greve hem what he myghte.

Not I how longe or short it was bitwene
This purpos and that day they fighten mente;
But on a day wel armed, brighte, and shene,
Ector and many a worthi wight out wente,
With spere in honde and bigge bowes bente;
And in the berd, withouten lenger lette,
Hire fomen in the feld anon hem mette.

The longe day, with speres sharpe igrounde,
With arwes, dartes, swerdes, maces felle,
They fighte and bringen hors and man to grounde,
And with hire axes out the braynes quelle.
But in the laste shour, soth for to telle,
The folk of Troie hemselven so mysledden
That with the worse at nyght homward they
    fledden.

                                    [IV, 29–49]

The heroic vision is thus in this poem exposed to and limited by the tragic perspective of human history.

In the *Knight's Tale* the epic style and its concomitant ethos have their freest expression in Chaucer. Here Chaucer for once subordinates the courtly-love motif to the epic.[8] There are good reasons to believe that the tale was composed in substantially its present form, as a separate work, before the *Canterbury Tales*. If so, it was Chaucer's only complete, free-standing, unqualified treatment of the noble life, comparable to *Sir Gawain and the Green Knight*. If there is some doubt as to how seriously Chaucer takes the two young rivals Palamon and Arcite, there is no question that he takes Theseus seriously. The poem is a statement of ultimate belief in royal government and in the higher order of which it is a copy. "What maketh this but Juppiter, the kyng, / That is prince and cause of alle thyng . . .?" (3036–3037).

By putting it at the head of the *Canterbury Tales* Chaucer shows how deeply his own sympathies—or his sense of respect—were ultimately bound up with its ethos. But he put it into the *Canterbury Tales* nevertheless, and at that point may have added some of the flickerings of irony which critics persist in finding in it. In any event, the damage was done. The meaning of the tale is qualified in the new context. Apart from the juxtaposition of tales, a powerful basis for irony in the form of the *Canterbury Tales* is that it is a series narrated by different characters. The meaning of each tale is thus potentially qualified by our consideration of the special leanings and interests of the teller. The tale of Palamon and Arcite is assigned to a "verray, parfit, gentil knyght," a noble man of mature years, which both fixes its class orientation and suggests a certain nostalgia. It is followed by the disrespectful tales of the Miller and the Reeve, which in some ways parody it. They come nowhere near damaging it, but, permanently connected to it, they do not leave it the same.

Chaucer does not go back to romantic epic or epic romance after the *Troilus* and the *Knight's Tale* except in parody, but he does have a fling at a related mode: the romance, Arthurian or oriental, of magic and marvels. To look back at the multifariousness of the *House of Fame* once again, one would have imagined that

Chaucer could well have given himself up to this mode. The *House of Fame* is full of marvelous gimmicks, hugely enjoyed. What more magic steed than the Golden Eagle with its promise of love-tidings? What more exotic and enchanted places than the successive settings of that poem: the temple of glass, the mysterious desert, the hill of ice, the pinnacled abode of Fame, made all of beryl, and the revolving house of rumor, made all of varicolored twigs? Chaucer seems to have followed out later every one of the starts made in the *House of Fame,* but the results with this one are surprisingly meager. There is some magic, but not much of an atmosphere of the magical, in the *Franklin's Tale.* The *Wife of Bath's Tale* makes touching use of the idea of magic. In the context of the teller's sense of the loss of her youth and beauty, the magic transformation of the old hag into a young and fair lady is very gently suggested to be wish-fulfillment. But otherwise Chaucer is almost fidgety about the Celtic fairy atmosphere. His charming opening picture of the elf-queen and her jolly company is soon rent by the joking at the expense of begging friars. The rest of the fairy story is weighed down with the hag's Ovidian exemplum and sententious lecturing on *gentillesse* and poverty—which the tale survives very well, but not the magic nor the marvelous.

Chaucer seems even less at home in the Eastern atmosphere of the *Squire's Tale.* Had Milton's *penseroso* been able to

> . . . call up him that left half told
> The story of Cambuscan bold,

he might have found Chaucer quite unwilling to go on with it. The poem begins attractively enough, though the inordinate space given to repeated self-conscious remarks about rhetoric might give us pause. What is the meaning of this much interruption of the narrative? As the poem progresses, propelled by the exotic interest of the knight's arrival on his flying steed of brass, with his magic gifts, we are nevertheless aware that it is proceeding against some resistance. There is a certain woodenness in the endstopped lines, the repetitive and sententious character of passage after passage, as in fact the plot limps to a standstill (about verse 189) and then takes no significant turn for some hundreds of verses. At length Canacee finds her falcon and begins to listen to her story of unfaithfulness in love. We are, in short, out of the magical realm, and back to what, for Chaucer-lovers, is almost too familiar: Dido's lament in the *House of Fame,* the complaint of *Anelida,* and the romantic pathos of the legends of *Good Women.* Chaucer's odd confusion of the characters' names at the end of the fragment may be the final symptom of his dying interest. The peculiar clumsiness with which this oriental romance is handled by a great artist has prompted a number of comic interpretations at the expense of the tale's teller, abetted as usual by the Canterbury context.[9] Whether or not Chaucer's failure to complete the tale can be blamed on the Squire, the fact remains that the exotic magic leaks out of it early; oriental romance finally succumbs either to irony or to boredom.

In tracking out and sorting the varieties of Chaucer's romances we have come again and again upon the note of pathos. It is a subject which has been widely observed and admired in Chaucer, but it has not been adequately studied. Yet it must be by all odds the most persistent alternative to irony that Chaucer felt, so persistent that no account of Chaucer's character and stance would be complete without recognizing it. But dealing critically with pathos is a tricky business, since pathos is, to an extraordinary degree, relative to individual taste and sensibility.[10] One man's tenderness is another man's mawkishness. One generation is taught to weep, another to hold back the tears.

How shall we interpret and evaluate the pathetic Chaucer? Ideally we need first a consecutive account of the pathetic mode in earlier poetry, both religious and secular, Latin and vernacular, against which we might measure, at least comparatively, the quality and intensity of Chaucer's feeling. Pathos is a latent possibility, at least, in most periods and genres of literature; it is a presence in medieval literature as early as the time of Anselm of Canterbury and Bernard of Clairvaux. Considering the openings for it in pious subject matter —the sacrifice of Isaac, the slaughter of the Innocents, the Nativity, the Passion, the life and miracles of the Virgin Mary, the legends of such saints as Elisabeth and Paula—early medieval literature has relatively few heavily pathetic passages.[11] But there is a real shift of sensibility—of which the rise of Franciscanism may be more a symptom than a cause—toward the middle of the thirteenth century; we need particularly a close study of the change in religious feelings that produces in this period the fully pathetic version of the life of Christ found in the iconography traced by Mâle and in the *Meditations* of the pseudo-Bonaventura.[12] We would find Chaucer, I think, in the full tide of this typically late-medieval sentimentalization of religious feeling, and it is possible that for the England of his time, and for some centuries thereafter, he is a cultural land-mark in the breadth and depth to which the feeling runs.[13]

For our present purposes, we shall have to be content with the more limited appraisal of Chaucer's pathos that we can get from comparing his different works. Pathos falls across both his romantic and religious poems, and no doubt its powerful expression in such works as the *Clerk's Tale* derives from the fusion of both streams. Griselda is both a Christian mother and a legendary heroine. It is interesting to observe, then (assuming always that our rough chronology is correct), that Chaucer's early works in both genres do not show anything suggesting extremes of pathos. *An ABC* is a translation from De Deguileville, and both the choice of the piece and the closeness of the transla-tion may indicate some tendency on Chaucer's part, before the *Canterbury Tales* years, to lean toward a mariology that is reverent and tender but not senti-mental. The crucified Jesus and sorrowing Mary have little space in *An ABC;* what pathos there is, rather, is generated more by the sinning speaker's own stance as an erring child of God:

> Glorius mayde and mooder, which that nevere
> Were bitter, neither in erthe nor in see,
> But ful of swetnesse and of merci evere,
> Help that my Fader be not wroth with me.
> Spek thou, for I ne dar not him ysee,
> So have I doon in erthe, allas the while!
> That certes, but if thou my soccour bee,
> To stink eterne he wole my gost exile.

[49–56]

The *Second Nun's Tale,* similarly a close translation, is even more continent, and asks of us neither sigh nor tear as we witness the martyr St. Cecelia's perfection both in courage and in doctrine.

I have several times mentioned the long lament of Dido in the *House of Fame.* It is by no means certain why Chaucer made it so long; it can be read as merely a rhetorical exercise, perhaps meant to be comic.[14] Within it is practice in the love-complaint mode and surely an attempt at pathos:

> "Allas!" quod she, "my swete herte,
>   Have pitee on my sorwes smerte,
>   And slee mee not! goo noght awey!
>   O woful Dido, wel-away!"
>   Quod she to hirselve thoo.
>   "O Eneas, what wol ye doo?
>   O that your love, ne your bond
>   That ye have sworn with your ryght hond,
>   Ne my crewel deth," quod she,
>   "May holde yow stille here with me!
>   O haveth of my deth pitee!
>   Iwys, my dere herte, ye
>   Knowen ful wel that never yit,
>   As ferforth as I hadde wyt,
>   Agylte [I] yow in thoght ne dede.
>   O, have ye men such godlyhede
>   In speche, and never a del of trouthe?
>   Allas, that ever hadde routhe
>   Any woman on any man!
>   Now see I wel, and telle kan,
>   We wrechched wymmen konne noon art;
>   For certeyn, for the more part,

> Thus we be served everychone.
> How sore that ye men konne groone,
> Anoon as we have yow receyved,
> Certaynly we ben deceyvyd!
> For, though your love laste a seson,
> Wayte upon the conclusyon,
> And eke how that ye determynen,
> And for the more part diffynen."

[315–344]

Whatever Chaucer's intent here, the mixture of other modes in the speech, especially the scholastic, squelches whatever sympathy is generated. Furthermore we see here a hint of a quality that may be found in other specimens of Chaucerian pathos—a lack of background, of context, within which the powerful feeling might have taken on more local solidity and justification.

The occasions for pathos are multiplied by as many good women as there are in the *Legend of Good Women,* but here again we find remarkably little sustained pathos, either achieved or attempted. There are a few tentative fingerings of the theme of suffering children, which will later become a very fount of Chaucerian tenderness. Thus Tisbe apostrophizes her father before she kills herself:

> "And now, ye wrechede jelos fadres oure,
> We that whilom were children youre,
> We preyen yow, withouten more envye,
> That in o grave yfere we moten lye,
> Sith love hath brought us to this pitous ende.
> And ryghtwis God to every lovere sende,
> That loveth trewely, more prosperite

Than evere yit had Piramus and Tisbe! . . ."
[900–907]

In the legend of Dido, Chaucer picks up the Ovidian suggestion that Dido was pregnant:

"I am with childe, and yeve my child his lyf!
Mercy, lord! have pite in your thought!"
[1323–1324]

In the legend of Hypermnestra, the daughter is made the victim of her wicked father. In the characterization of Lucrece we can see touches of the Griselda type of humble, wifely chastity; but she accepts the violence done her with Roman stoicism. Her account of the rape is told almost entirely in indirect discourse, so that although Chaucer tells us that

Al hadde folkes hertes ben of stones,
Hyt myght have maked hem upon hir rewe. . . .
[1841–1842]

the account is too masked and compressed to summon our tears. The rape of Philomela leads to similarly condensed pathetics.

The note of pathos in most of these accounts is summoned by Chaucer not only for unrequited love—the conventional cue for complaint—but more often for defenseless weakness against a brutal, masculine world. Without a rich context, these anecdotes seem to be drawing in part on stock response, on some easy source of feeling in the audience—"pitee renneth soone in gentil herte." When Chaucer provides such passages an adequate context, however, they draw from deeper wells of feeling and take on deeper meaning. One of the most successful touches of pathos in Chaucer, both poetically and strategically, is the beginning of the death speech of Arcite in the *Knights' Tale:*

> "Naught may the woful spirit in myn herte
> Declare o point of alle my sorwes smerte
> To yow, my lady, that I love moost;
> Bit I biquethe the servyce of my goost
> To yow aboven every creature,
> Syn that my lyf may no lenger dure.
> Allas, the wo! allas, the peynes stronge,
> That I for yow have suffred, and so longe!
> Allas, the deeth! allas, myn Emelye!
> Allas, departynge of oure compaignye!
> Allas, myn hertes queene! allas, my wyf!
> Myn hertes lady, endere of my lyf!
> What is this world? what asketh men to have?
> Now with his love, now in his colde grave
> Allone, withouten any compaignye.
> Fare wel, my sweete foo, myn Emelye!
> And softe taak me in youre armes tweye,
> For love of God, and herkneth what I seye. . . ."
>
> [2765–2782]

Here the powerful feeling is contained, both fore and aft, by the narrator's prosaic and medical acceptance of Arcite's death. Meanwhile we have been exposed to a pathos as deep as human doubt can go. "What is this world, what asketh men to have?" The fact that the whole of this rich poem devotes itself to finding an acceptable answer to the question somehow validates the feeling and supports us in our temporary surrender.

But the glimpse of man "in his colde grave" should remind us that not all such feeling in the late Middle Ages was so contained and supported in its pathos.

Huizinga remarks that the new preoccupation with Death in the period is not a form of asceticism or religiosity, but rather the reverse.[15] It presumes a worship of the living flesh and a desperate pessimism as to the hereafter. It proclaims the weakening of faith. Chaucer never falls into the blacker stages of the fifteenth-century mood (though he approaches them in the plague and murder scenes of the *Pardoner's Tale*). But I wonder whether the extreme pathos of the Hugelino episode, of the *Clerk's, Physician's, Prioress's,* and *Man of Law's Tales*—if we set them beside the confident dignity of *An ABC* and the *Second Nun's Tale*—do not show a wavering of morale along with the undeniable increase in poetic power and religious feeling. For the pathos of defenseless weakness can be based on a kind of pessimism that sees in the world malignity without cause and without cure; justice perverted; protection uncertain. The miracle of the Blessed Virgin, the need for divine intercessory tenderness, long antedates Chaucer's time. But when it comes as relief from a strain that has begun to grow intolerable, it brings a new accession of pathos.

The whole subject of suffering children is introduced between the two groups of poems we are comparing. The turning of the mature Chaucer to the subject of children is itself a symptom of something. Children, to all intents and purposes, were not recognized in art or literature until the late thirteenth century,[16] and their discovery is coincident with the shift in religious feeling we have noted above. In the absence of statistics we cannot attribute it to a lessening of infant mortality —more likely there was a rise, in a period of plague, famine, war, and depression. In fact, nearly all of Chaucer's children exist, not to live out their childlike

lives, but to suffer death, or the threat of death. It is
true, as D. S. Brewer points out, that this is a fact of
fourteenth-century life;[17] but it was also a fact of thirteenth-century life, and that century was peculiarly
untroubled by death. The direction in which this sen-
timent is moving is well illustrated in the fifteenth century in Antoine de la Sale's *Le Réconfort de Madame
du Fresne:*

> But the child, who thought, after the guards' con-
> soling words, that he was being taken toward the
> fortress, when he saw that they were going toward
> Mont Réont, was frightened more than ever. He now
> began to weep and despair and said to Thomas, the
> leader of the guards: "Oh, Thomas, my friend, you
> take me away to die, you take me away to die. Alas,
> you take me away to die, Thomas, you take me
> away to die. Alas, my lord father, I shall die. Alas,
> my lady mother, I shall die. I shall die! Alas, alas,
> alas, I shall die, die, die, die!" And crying thus and
> weeping, looking before and behind and around him,
> he saw me, woe unto me!, with your coat of arms
> which I wore, and when he saw me, he called aloud,
> as loud as he could. And he said to me: "Ah,
> Chastel, my friend, I shall die! Alas! My friend, I
> shall die!" And when I heard him cry thus, then like
> dead I fell to the ground. And according to orders I
> was carried after him and there by many men was
> held until he met his end. And when he was set
> down on the mount, there was there a friar who, by
> beautiful words of hope in the grace of God, little
> by little confessed him and absolved him from his
> little sins. And because he could not take death
> willingly, they had to hold his head and bind his

arms and legs so that the legs were bruised by the iron down to the bones. . . .[18]

Chaucer does not go this far, of course, yet it is worthwhile plotting his position on the curve. Theodore Spencer, in a paper that deserves to be better remembered, has already called our attention to the comparison between Chaucer's and Dante's renderings of the Ugolino episode (*Inferno* XXXIII).[19] If Dante's generates pity and terror, Chaucer's generates only pity. A softness has entered in. Comparatively, Chaucer is sentimental. Where Dante's Ugolino feels a grief so stonily deep that it cuts off both speech and tears,

> Io non piangeva, si dentro impietrai. . . .
>
> [49]

[I did not weep; inside I turned to stone]

Chaucer's Hugelino complains and weeps:

> "Allas!" quod he, "allas, that I was wroght!"
> Therwith the teeris fillen from his yen.
>
> [2429–2430]

The following stanza is Chaucer's addition:

> His yonge sone, that thre yeer was of age,
> Unto hym seyde, "Fader, why do ye wepe?
> Whanne wol the gayler bryngen oure potage?
> Is there no morsel breed that ye do kepe?
> I am so hungry that I may nat slepe.
> Now wolde God that I myghte slepen evere!
> Thanne sholde nat hunger in my wombe crepe;
> There is no thyng, save breed, that me were levere."
>
> [2431–2438]

The iron terror of Dante's concluding line—*poscia, più che il dolor, potè il digiuno,* "then fasting had more power than grief"—is lost in Chaucer's conclusion: "Hymself, despeired, eek for hunger starf."

Of the remaining four pieces that concern us, one needs little discussion. The *Physician's Tale* has not been widely praised in recent years, partly because of the hard-boiledness of our taste, but also because the tale lacks adquate underpinnings for the extremes of pathos that it attempts to engage us in. We know nothing of the Physician that would attract us to joining his feelings, and the tale generates neither the characterization nor the sense of a cosmos that in the *Troilus* or the *Knight's Tale* make the pathos acceptable. It is the gratuitousness of it that finally palls. The heroine is a textbook example of medieval secular virtue and she is done in by an equally pure vice:

> "O mercy, deere fader!" quod this mayde,
> And with that word she bothe hir armes layde
> Aboute his nekke, as she was wont to do.
> The teeris bruste out of hir eyen two,
> And seyde, "Goode fader, shal I dye?
> Is ther no grace, is ther no remedye?"
>> "No certes, deere doghter myn," quod he.
>> "Thanne yif me leyser, fader myn," quod she,
> "My deeth for to compleyne a litel space;
> For pardee, Jepte yaf his doghter grace
> For to compleyne, er he hir slow, allas!
> And, God it woot, no thyng was hir trespas,
> But for she ran hir fader first to see,
> To welcome hym with greet solempnitee."
> And with that word she fil aswowne anon,
> And after, whan hir swownyng is agon,

She riseth up, and to hir fader sayde,
"Blissed be God, that I shal dye a mayde!
Yif me my deeth, er that I have a shame;
Dooth with youre child youre wyl, a Goddes name!"
[231–250]

To make matters worse, the narrative style has such an unwonted flaccidity and the few essential details of plot are handled so vaguely[20] as to rob the tale further of any power it might have had to make us suspend disbelief.

The *Prioress's Tale*, on the other hand, is one of Chaucer's most moving poems. Some of its power must be due to the fact that the pathos is extraordinarily well enfolded in the characterization of the Prioress and allows even the most hard-boiled of us to take just as much of it as he wishes.[21] The rest can be attributed to the delicate, feminine, maternal nun who tells the tale. This characterization, however, does not depend entirely on pilgrimage dramatics, on our knowing the Prioress from Chaucer's *General Prologue;* it is woven deeply into the style of the tale: in the consistent self-identification of the speaker with childlikeness; the repeated emphasis on weakness, simplicity, and on the diminutive (a *litel child,* a *litel scole,* his *litel book,* his *litel body*); the adoption of a simple diction and syntax for the narrator as well as for the child; the use of repetitions in passages and within phrases, giving the effect of simplicity; the use, repeatedly, of simply contrasts and distinctions to the same effect. Like the *Physician's Tale,* the poem turns on an elementary contrast between tenderness and violence, but the feel of tenderness is made far more substantial and appealing. Furthermore, the element of violence, the malignity and punishment of the Jews, instead of standing quite apart from tenderness, is hinged to it in the emotional system of the tale: in one stanza the image of the child's body thrown in the privy, in the next stanza the procession of the white Lamb celestial; in the same three verses the provost

> . . . herieth Crist that is of hevene king
> And eek his mooder, honour of mankynde,
> And after that the Jewes leet he bynde.
>
> [618–620]

In four successive verses spanning a stanza break:

> Therefore with wilde hors he dide hem drawe,
> And after that he heng hem by the lawe.
>
> Upon this beere ay lith this innocent
> Beforn the chief auter, whil masse laste. . . .
>
> [633–636]

I do not wish to enter the controversy over the Prioress's anti-Semitism or other alleged flaws in her character. But surely Chaucer is touching something true here, in these contrasts, about the kinship of pathos and violence as extremes of feeling. Their coupling, whether or not it seems grotesque, adds validity to each; and this may be, at least in part, why the poem can be read both as successful pathos and as an exposure (conscious or unconscious) of the brutality which lies beneath it.

If the success of the pathetic style in the *Prioress's Tale* is a matter of total fitness, total decorum, perhaps what bothers some readers of the *Clerk's Tale* is not the relatively restrained pathos it employs, but that pathos threatens not to fit. The poem is extremely dense and powerful in its design and extremely well fitted to the ethos of the speaker. But the speaker is a lean, philosophical man, and the design is clear, sharp, and uncompromising.[22] The uncompromising virtue of Griselda (even with her resemblances to Lucrece and Virginia) fits this design better than do the extremes of pathos. Fortunately the few stanzas of it, centering mostly around the loss and recovery of her children, hardly mar the poem.

The case is far worse in the *Man of Law's Tale;* after the *House of Fame* this is surely Chaucer's most tantalizing and exasperating poem. Tantalizing because it contains individual passages of the most affecting beauty; exasperating because so much of the rest of its feeling is unavailable except to the most willing hearts. This is not to say that the *Man of Law's Tale* would not have been prized by Chaucer's contemporaries. It must be included in that roll of serious and elevating works in the high style on which Chaucer's reputation was largely to rest in the next two centuries. Yet is has not survived as well as have other of the pious tales of the same drift, and some answer must be sought in the tale itself.

Unlike the *Prioress's* and *Clerk's Tales,* the *Man of Law's Tale,* although suitable to him, has no deeply necessary congruity with what we know of the character of the speaker. It cannot be said to represent anything that confirms or combines richly with his nature; it shows, indeed, some sign of having been assigned to the Man of Law at the last minute. If its barren stretches illustrate Chaucer's observation that the Man of Law "semed bisier than he was," the joke is a heavy one at best. Chaucer heightened the religious flavor and suppressed some of the melodrama found in the story he was adapting, and it looks as if he originally intended it to stand on its own feet, without a framing of dramatics or irony, as a kind of saint's legend.

Professor Alfred David has put his finger on an essential difference between the pessimism of the *Man of Law's Tale* and that of the *Knight's Tale:* "The dominant philosophical influence" on the former "is not *De consolatione philosophiae* but *De contemptu mundi.*"[23] Thus the religiosity of the *Man of Law's Tale* is deeper, and it makes a more naked, more naive, less philosophical appeal when it invokes divine providence. As art it calls for a far greater initial contribution of stock response from its audience. Like the *Clerk's Tale,* its plot is repetitive; but somehow its power is not cumulative. Like the *Prioress's Tale,* its color is black and white, but the contrasts are not arranged in any convincing pattern. The rhetoric of the poem is put out at a pressure that in this context would require the Pardoner's skill to bring off. Some of its flights rise so suddenly out of the mediocre recital of the plot as to suggest that the poet is coming to the rescue, sensing that the narrative itself is not pulling its own weight.[24] Then we come upon a passage like Constance's prayer on the beach, with its climactic invocation to the Virgin Mary:

> Wepen bothe yonge and olde in al that place
> Whan that the kyng this cursed lettre sente,
> And Custance, with a deedly pale face,
> The ferthe day toward hir ship she wente.
> But nathelees she taketh in good entente
> The wyl of Crist, the knelynge on the stronde,
> Se seyde, "Lord, ay welcome be thy sonde!
>
> "He that me kepte fro the false blame
> While I was on the lond amonges yow,

He kan me kepe from harm and eek fro shame
In salte see, althogh I se noght how.
As strong as evere he was, he is yet now.
In hym triste I, and in his mooder deere,
That is to me my seyl and eek my steere."

Hir litel child lay wepyng in hir arm,
And knelynge, pitously to hym she seyde,
"Pees, litel sone, I wol do thee noon harm."
With that hir coverchief of hir heed she breyde,
And over his litel eyen she it leyde,
And in hir arm she lulleth it ful faste,
And into hevene hire eyen up she caste.

    "Mooder," quod she, "and mayde bright, Marie,
Sooth is that thurgh wommanes eggement
Mankynde was lorn, and damned ay to dye,
For which thy child was on a croys yrent.
Thy blisful eyen sawe al his torment;
Thanne is ther no comparison bitwene
Thy wo and any wo man may sustene.

"Thow sawe thy child yslayn bifore thyne yen,
And yet now lyveth my litel child, parfay!
Now, lady bright, to whom alle woful cryen,
Thow glorie of wommanhede, thow faire may,
Thow haven of refut, brighte sterre of day,
Rewe on my child, that of thy gentillesse,
Rewest on every reweful in distresse."

[820–854]

The passage can hardly be read with a dry eye. It is
one of the greatest of Chaucer's lyrics, and we remain
grateful to him—even in the following stanza, where
he makes a palpable effort to squeeze for even more
tears.

The pathos in Chaucer, hedged about by its pious associations, is almost totally exempt from overt irony, except perhaps that of a cosmic kind, as in the *Troilus,* which reminds us that even this ineffable sadness and pity we feel is an attachment to the world. Perhaps that is why, finally, so much pathos is contained within the enveloping structure of the *Canterbury Tales.*

In dealing with Chaucer I have followed a method quite different from that in the two previous discussions, and I hope not to be misunderstood—particularly by readers new to Chaucer. I have not given due attention here to Chaucer's main achievements, for lack of space and because they have in any case been well celebrated elsewhere. Our rapid survey of some Chaucerian excursions outside of irony has, however, a celebratory effect: to confirm that Chaucer's crowning ironic stance, though highly original, was not inevitable but emerges from a lifetime of feeling and of coming to grips with the alternative value systems that his culture offered. He tried, he tested, he experimented, he compromised, and even had moments of pessimism and failure. We see that some moods came on him late, and others were abandoned early; that he may have been tempted here, and that he resisted temptation there. Apart from his perception and sympathy with life, Chaucer's great virtue is morale. It is a morale that is based, not on a doctrinaire conservatism, but on a felt acquaintance with all the alternatives.

"Poetry" as Frederick Pottle says, "cannot go wrong."[25] It is always related to history, for it is the very truest record of human sensibility. So poetry is always relevant. The question is, how does it connect? In making our survey of three poets at the same moment of history, we have found not only three different responses, but also three rather different ways in which poetry can relate to history, three kinds of relatedness between poetic art and a culture in crisis. One poet refines out, in his art, all of the contemporary except the ultimate moral issues, and reclothes them in terms that defend them from the accidental and the local. Another poet immerses himself and his poem in the moving current of history, from which both emerge with the marks of crisis upon them. The third is somewhere in between, involved yet objective, detached yet sympathetically moved. These three are great poets, and their response to their own culture is deeper and truer than other men's. Studying through them the relation of poetry to history, we learn something about the responses of men to history as well.

NOTES TO CHAPTER I

1. See, for instance, the two volumes of *Daedalus, Proceedings of the American Academy of Arts and Sciences* 98, no. 3 (1969): *The Future of the Humanities*; and 99, no. 2 (1970): *Theory in Humanistic Studies*; also J. Mitchell Morse, "The Case for Irrelevance," *College English* 30 (1968): 201–211, and the issue of *College English* 30, no. 8, (1969).

2. Roy Harvey Pearce, *Historicism Once More: Problems & Occasions for the American Scholar* (Princeton: Princeton Univ. Press, 1969), p. vii.

3. See René Wellek and Austin Warren, *Theory of Literature* (New York: Harcourt, Brace, 1949), which well represents the New Criticism in its institutional form, as summarized in this paragraph. Chapter 12 deals partly with the ontological status of literature.

4. A more extended critique of the New Criticism in these terms is made by Pearce, "Historicism Once More," *Kenyon Review* 20 (1958): 558–566, reprinted in his collection of the same name, pp. 8–17; cf. also Robert Weimann, "Past Significance and Present Meaning in Literary History," *New Literary History* 1 (1969): esp. 93–98; and John Gerber, "Literature—Our Untamable Discipline," *College English* 28 (1967): 351–358.

5. The ahistorical bent of the first three seems to me self-evident. But since the "exegetical" approach to medieval studies sometimes comes with an air of superior historicity—as approaching medieval literature as the medievals saw it rather than with modern (and thus with anachronistic) assumptions—I should explain that the approach seems to me ahistorical in two related ways. Its "medievalism" has almost no nuances; that is, it tends to posit a uniform set of ideas, and by implication a homogenous culture, over a thousand years of history in which historians of art, music, philosophy, etc., see a great diversity; secondly, its assumption that the bulk of medieval literature is Christian and didactic in a specific way leads to a method that is essentially the same as that of the other ahistorical approaches: a search for recurrent patterns, which (whether rooted in prehistory, biology, the collective unconscious, or in Christian revelation) are regarded a priori as permanently valid, and are thus of little historical interest.

6. See Leo Marx, "American Studies—A Defense of an

Unscientific Method," *New Literary History* 1 (1969): 75–90, and the references in his note 2.

7. My favorite students of style are both medievalists and both profoundly interested in cultural history: Erich Auerbach, as in *Mimesis: The Representation of Reality in Western Literature* [1946], trans. Willard R. Trask (Princeton: Princeton Univ. Press, 1953); and Leo Spitzer, as in *Linguistics and Literary History: Essays in Stylistics* (Princeton: Princeton Univ. Press, 1948). A bibliography of Auerbach's works appears in his *Literary Language and Its Public in Late Latin Antiquity and in the Middle Ages*, trans. Ralph Manheim, Bollingen Series 74 (New York: Pantheon, 1965), pp. 395–405. There is as yet no complete bibliography of the very prolific Spitzer; a selected bibliography is appended to the obituary article by René Wellek on Spitzer as critic and theorist in *Comparative Literature* 12 (1960): 310–330, with supplement in volume 13 (1961): 378–379. For modern English stylistics in general, see Richard W. Bailey and Dolores M. Burton, S.N.D., *English Stylistics: A Bibliography* (Cambridge, Mass.: M.I.T. Press, 1968) with periodic supplements in the journal *Style*. On linguistics and literature, see the article by Samuel Levin and Seymour Chatman in *Current Trends in Linguistics*, ed. W. Bright et al. ('S-Gravenhage: Mouton [announced for 1971]); Seymour Chatman, ed., *Literary Style: A Symposium* (London: Oxford Univ. Press, 1971), esp. the article by Richard Ohmann, "Speech, Action, and Style"; and D. C. Freeman, ed., *Linguistics and Literary Style* (New York: Holt, Rinehart, and Winston, 1970).

8. The matter is of course a complicated one, and our notions and definitions of period style are continually being refined. See the issue of *New Literary History* 1, no. 2 (Winter, 1970), entitled "A Symposium on Periods." The liveliness of this new journal is symptomatic of the current interest of our subject.

9. See Wellek and Warren, *Theory of Literature*, pp. 117–123; E. H. Gombrich, *In Search of Cultural History* (Oxford: Clarendon, 1969) offers a broad critique of *Geistesgeschichte*.

10. See Spitzer, *Linguistics and Literary History*, chaps. 1–4.

11. Johan Huizinga's term "autumn" or "waning" is the mildest epithet I have found to describe the general setting of the period. *The Age of Adversity* is the title of a recent study by Robert E. Lerner (Ithaca: Cornell Univ. Press, 1968). Norman E. Cantor remarks of the fourteenth and fifteenth

centuries: "In France, England, Germany, and Flanders it is the death agonies of medieval civilization which predominate. . . ." (*Medieval History* [New York: Macmillan, 1963], p. 577). In a textbook more restrained in its approach, Jeffrey Burton Russell nevertheless comments, vis-à-vis economic conditions, "The period from 1349 to 1470 was a Golden Age only for bacteria" (*Medieval Civilization* [New York: John Wiley, 1968], p. 559). F. R. H. DuBoulay, in the first chapter of his *An Age of Ambition: English Society in the Late Middle Ages* (London: Nelson, 1970) announces an attack on the "Myth of Decline," but there is little in his study to change the prevailing view of the last half of the fourteenth century. In his chapter entitled "The Apparatus of Religion," moreover, he admits that "it was on all hands an age of special anxiety. Every literary and artistic form tells us so. The pestilence and sudden death which actually brought social betterment to the survivors, the social mobility and conflict that resulted, the need for thousands of families to adjust themselves in one way or another under the lowering clouds of sudden mortality, brought with them also a sense of insecurity and terror." (p. 145).

12. Brief resumés on the economic state of Europe will be found in Jacques Heers, *L'Occident aux XIVe et XVe siècles: aspects économiques et sociaux*, 2d ed. (Paris: Presses Universitaires, 1966), pp. 104–107, and in Ruggiero Romano and Alberto Tenenti, *Die Grundlegung der modernen Welt: Spätmittelalter, Renaissance, Reformation* (Frankfurt am Main: Fischer, 1967), pp. 9–47 ("Die 'Krise' des 14, Jahrhunderts"); on England see May McKisack, *The Fourteenth Century: 1307–1399*, vol. 5 in *The Oxford History of England*, (Oxford: Clarendon, 1959), pp. 328–348.

13. See R. B. Dobson, ed., *The Peasants' Revolt of 1381* (London: Macmillan, 1970), p. 375. This is an excellent collection of original documents in modern English translation: a good general account of the revolt is C. Oman, *The Great Revolt of 1381* [orig. pub. 1906], new ed. by E. B. Fryde (Oxford: Clarendon, 1969).

14. Dobson, *Peasants' Revolt*, p. 311.

15. May McKisack, *The Fourteenth Century*, p. 423; cf. p. 384: "The first and least sensational of these attacks resulted in the substitution, in 1371, of lay for clerical ministers of state; the second, in 1376, in the impeachment of the king's chamberlain and a number of lesser officials; the third, in 1381, in the murder of the chancellor and treasurer and

the indiscriminate massacre of certain officers of the law and minor civil servants."

16. Gervase Mathew, *The Court of Richard II* (London: John Murray, 1968), p. 114; cf. A. R. Myers, *England in the Late Middle Ages* (Harmondsworth: Penguin, 1952), pp. xiii–xiv. On politics in the reign of Richard II, see Anthony Steel, *Richard II* (Cambridge: Cambridge Univ. Press, 1941), and R. H. Jones, *The Royal Policy of Richard II: Absolutism in the Later Middle Ages* (New York: Barnes and Noble, 1968).

17. Dobson, *Peasants' Revolt*, p. 374.

18. Gordon Leff, *Heresy in the Later Middle Ages: The Relation of Heterodoxy to Dissent c. 1250–c. 1450*, 2 vols. (Manchester: Manchester Univ. Press), I, 14.

19. On Wyclif and Lollardy, see Leff, *Heresy in the Late Middle Ages,* II, 494–558.

20. Leff, *Heresy in the Late Middle Ages*, I, 31. The early-fifteenth-century Margery Kempe is more notably histrionic, or hysterical, than any fourteenth-century English mystic; W. A. Pantin, *The English Church in the Fourteenth Century* (Cambridge: Cambridge Univ. Press, 1955), considers her, however, "a product of fourteenth-century conditions" (p. 256), and "a creditable specimen of the devout lay person in the later Middle Ages" (p. 261).

21. Joan Evans, *English Art: 1307–1461* (Oxford: Clarendon, 1949), p. 74. "It is a remarkable fact that it has been possible to give a continuous history of the early Perpendicular style without reference to the national disasters which occurred in its years of growth. Yet these were so great that it seems miraculous that they did not leave a greater scar upon the art of England." On the art of Richard II's reign, see *ibid.*, pp. 82–86, 100–105; also Margaret Rickert, *Painting in Britain: The Middle Ages* (London: Penguin, 1954), pp. 165–189; Mathew, *Court of Richard II*, chaps. 5 and 10 (the latter chapter contains interesting and original remarks on some remnants of didactic "provincial" art related to the themes of *Piers Plowman*); Lawrence Stone, *Sculpture in Britain: The Middle Ages* (Harmondsworth: Penguin, 1955), pp. 177–195.

22. Émile Mâle, *L'Art réligieux du XIIᵉ au XVIIIᵉ siècle* (Paris: Colin [1945], repr. 1961), p. 91, my translation.

23. Émile Mâle, *L'Art réligieux de la fin du moyen âge en France: etude sur l'iconographie du moyen âge et sur ses*

sources d'inspiration, 5th ed. (Paris: Colin, 1949), pp. 85–86, my translation.

24. Mâle, *L'Art réligieux de la fin du moyen âge*, pp. 122–132, 146–150, 157–221.

25. Johan Huizinga, *The Waning of the Middle Ages: A Study of the Forms of Life, Thought and Art in France and the Netherlands in the XIVth and XVth Centuries* [1919; Engl. trans. 1924] (London: Arnold, 1937), p. 240.

26. Huizinga, *Waning of the Middle Ages*, pp. 126, 189. On the period generally, Huizinga is still our principal authority. On the literature see also Italo Siciliano, *François Villon et les thèmes poétiques du moyen âge* (Paris: Colin, 1934), esp. pp. 115–199; on the imagery of Death, see Mâle, *L'Art réligieux de la fin du moyen âge*, pp. 347–389. It may be worth noting that the Dance of Death is a well-documented motif in English art of the fifteenth century, and that the earlier, related theme of the Three Living and Three Dead appears plentifully in the surviving English mural paintings of the fourteenth century. See the two articles by Ethel Carleton Williams, "The Dance of Death in Painting and Sculpture in the Middle Ages," *Journal of the British Archaeological Association*, 3d ser., I (1937): 237–239, and "Mural Paintings of the Three Living and the Three Dead in England," *ibid.*, 7 (1942): 31–40.

27. Martin M. Crow and Clair C. Olson, *Chaucer Life-Records* (Oxford: Clarendon, 1966).

28. John S. P. Tatlock, *The Development and Chronology of Chaucer's Works*, Chaucer Society Pubs., 2d ser., 37 (London, 1907) is still the most authoritative single treatment of the chronology.

29. George Lyman Kittredge, *Chaucer and His Poetry* (Cambridge, Mass.: Harvard Univ. Press, 1915), p. 45.

30. E. Talbot Donaldson, "Chaucer the Pilgrim," *PMLA* 49 (1954): 935.

31. See, respectively, Crow and Olson, *Life-Records*, pp. 269, 364–369; 269–270; 343–347. Two of the articles of a recently discovered ordinance of Parliament in 1385 are of particular interest as regards Chaucer's giving up of his customs posts. As a result of an inquest, Parliament recommended to the King:

> Item les profitz de sa graunt custume et petit custume serrount grandement encruz sil luy plest que les custumez et aultrez officers appendantz aycellez soient ordeynez

> des bons et loyalx gentz par avys de son conseill et ses
> officers et nient par priere ne desir singuler, et remuablez
> selonc lour deserte; et qilz soient demouranuntz sur lour
> office sanz leutenantz ou attournez. . . .
>
> Item le subside dez laynes a luy grauntez et pelles
> lanutez poet graundement estre encruz sil luy plest suffrer
> que lez custumers, contrerollours et poysers porront estre
> ordenez des bonez et loyalx gentz par avys soun conseillers
> et ses officers et nient par singuler desir ne requeste, et
> remuablez selonck lour deserts, et demourauntz sur leur
> office en propre persone.

Since Chaucer was controller of both the wool custom and
subsidy and the petty custom at London at the time, he cannot
but have fallen under suspicion of neglect of his posts at the
very least, no matter what his deserts. See J. J. N. Palmer,
"The Impeachment of Michael de la Pole in 1386," *Bulletin
of the Institute of Historical Research* 42 (1969): 96–101;
idem, "The Parliament of 1385 and the Constitutional Crisis
of 1386," *Speculum* 46 (1971): esp. 483. The ordinance
is printed in the former of these, pp. 100–101.

32. In *Chaucer and the French Tradition: A Study in
Style and Meaning* (Berkeley: Univ. of California Press,
1957).

33. George Kane, *Piers Plowman: The Evidence for
Authorship* (London: Univ. of London, Athlone Press, 1965).

NOTES TO CHAPTER II

1. For the works of the *Pearl* poet I use the following edi-
tions: *Purity*, ed. Robert J. Menner, Yale Studies in English
61 (New Haven: Yale Univ. Press, 1920); *Pearl*, ed. E. V.
Gordon (Oxford: Clarendon, 1953); *Sir Gawain and the
Green Knight*, ed. J. R. R. Tolkien and E. V. Gordon, 2d ed.
rev. Norman Davis (Oxford: Clarendon, 1967); *Patience*,
ed. J. J. Anderson (Manchester, Manchester Univ. Press,
1969).

2. See respectively *Purity*, vv. 285–292, 303–308, 363–406,
947–972, 1215–1260, 1767–1792; *Patience*, vv. 137–232,
273–280.

3. Menner, ed. *Purity*, p. 67, remarks that "even here his
condemnation of wicked priests is quite different from the
violent denunciations of the author of *Piers Plowman*, since

he is careful to contrast impartially the behavior and reward of righteous priests . . . with the sin of those who are vile and hyprocritical."

4. See Carleton Brown, "The Author of the Pearl Considered in the Light of His Theological Opinions," *PMLA* 19 (1904): 115–153; René Wellek, "The *Pearl*: An Interpretation of the Middle English Poem," [orig. pub. 1933] in Robert J. Blanch, ed., *Sir Gawain and Pearl: Critical Essays* (Bloomington: Indiana Univ. Press, 1966), pp. 11–12, 24–33; Gordon, ed., *Pearl*, pp. xxiii–xxvii.

5. Cf. A. C. Spearing, "Symbolic and Dramatic Development in *Pearl*," *Modern Philology* 60 (1962): 11 [repr. *Blanch*, ed., *Sir Gawain and Pearl*, pp. 117–118.]

6. A study of the various meanings of the term "courtesy" as used by the poet will be found in D. S. Brewer, "Courtesy and the Gawain-Poet," in John Lawlor, ed., *Patterns of Love and Courtesy: Essays in Memory of C. S. Lewis* (London: Arnold, 1966), pp. 54–85 [repr. in Helaine Newstead, ed., *Chaucer and his Contemporaries* (Greenwich, Conn.: Fawcett, 1968), pp. 310–343].

7. Wendell Stacy Johnson, "The Imagery and Diction of *The Pearl*: Toward an Interpretation," *ELH* 20 (1953): 165 [repr. in Edward Vasta, ed., *Middle English Survey: Critical Essays* (Notre Dame, Ind.: Univ. of Notre Dame Press, 1965), p. 98]. Johnson's analysis has been challenged by P.M. Kean, *The Pearl: An Interpretation* (London: Routledge, 1967), pp. 83–84: ". . . the imagery of treasure, of the garden, of the plant in all its parts and aspects, of spices, wheat, and harvest, forms an inextricably linked whole; not brought together by the poet but joined by long traditional use. It is not, therefore, possible to interpret the poem as developing its themes through juxtaposition of contrasted groups of images; for example, by opposing the artificiality and non-organic quality of treasure and jewels to the natural imagery of the plant." However, Johnson's thesis is I think strongly supported by such passages as vv. 269–272:

> "For þat þou lesteȝ watȝ bot a rose
> Þat flowred and fayled as kynde hyt gef.
> Now þurz kynde of þe kyste þat hyt con close
> To a perle of prys hit is put in pref."

Though elsewhere allusion is made to the immortal rose (v. 906), the opposition in the present passage is clear.

8. So A. C. Cawley, ed. and trans., *Pearl, Sir Gawain and the Green Knight*, Everyman's Library 346 (London: Dent, 1962), p. xvi; Dorothy Everett, in *Essays on Middle English Literature*, ed. Patricia Kean (Oxford: Clarendon, 1955), remarks (p. 88): "The same stanza form, and the linking, are found elsewhere in Middle English, and in some lyrics in the Vernon MS. for instance, but nowhere else is there anything like this complex scheme, nor is the stanza handled with such mastery."

9. Donald R. Howard, "Structure and Symmetry in Sir Gawain," *Speculum* 39 (1964): 425; see also pp. 430–431; Dale B. J. Randall, "A Note on Structure in *Sir Gawain and the Green Knight*," *MLN* 71 (1956): 319.

10. This interpretation follows particularly upon Larry D. Benson's study of variation in the diction, syntax, structure, and meaning of *Sir Gawain*; see his *Art and Tradition in Sir Gawain and the Green Knight* (New Brunswick, N.J.: Rutgers Univ. Press, 1965), esp. pp. 126–166, 247–248.

11. Johnson, "Imagery," pp. 166–167; cf. p. 172; and C. A. Luttrell, "*Pearl*: Symbolism in a Garden Setting," in Blanch, ed., *Sir Gawain and Pearl*, pp. 82–84.

12. See the excellent treatment by Spearing, "Symbolic and Dramatic Development," pp. 1–12 [repr. Blanch, ed., *Sir Gawain and Pearl*, pp. 98–119], to which I am much indebted in this discussion.

13. Marie Borroff, in *Sir Gawain and the Green Knight: A Stylistic and Metrical Study* (New Haven: Yale Univ. Press, 1962), pp. 121–129, points out certain highly interesting characteristics of the narrating "eye," some of which clearly intensify the descriptive richness of the poem: "The narrator tends to see a given object or agent in relation to other objects or agents within a limited space. The resultant effect is one of fullness or crowding . . ." (p. 123); "Descriptive details . . . are frequently circumstantial, expressing temporary conditions or relationships. . . . The result, as with the narrator's treatment of space, is to people or crowd the scene" (p. 124). "He tends also to adopt the point of view of the character central in a given narrative passage as that character responds to the circumstances of the action. The result is vividness, but it is vividness of a special kind. When it is visual, it depends as much on the exact appropriateness of what is seen, by whom, and from where, as on the color, texture, or other intrinsic sensory or aesthetic qualities of the object" (p. 128).

154 NOTES TO CHAPTER II

14. So, notably, Francis Berry, "Sir Gawayne and the Grene Knight," in *The Age of Chaucer*, ed. Boris Ford (London: Pelican, 1954), pp. 156–158.

15. The effect of the verse-form has been so described by J. B. Bessinger, Jr., on the cover of the Caedmon recording [TC2024] of his reading of the poem with Marie Borroff. A general tension in the poem between "formal" and "primitive" elements is noted by Berry, "Sir Gawayne," pp. 151–153; it is finely described in greater detail by William Goldhurst, "The Green and the Gold: The Major Theme of *Gawain and the Green Knight*," *College English* 20 (1958–59): 61–65.

16. P. B. Taylor, " 'Blysse and blunder,' Nature and Ritual in *Sir Gawain and the Green Knight*," *English Studies* 50 (1969): 165–175, begins at the same point but offers quite a different interpretation: "the focus of the story is on the extension and consequences of [Gawain's] blunder, which is misuse of heroic, or courtly, ritual" (p. 166).

17. Harvey Cox, *The Feast of Fools: A Theological Essay on Festival and Fantasy* (Cambridge, Mass.: Harvard Univ. Press, 1969), pp. 22–23.

18. Borroff, *Sir Gawain*, p. 121: "The narrator tends to see actions, whether major or minor, as reciprocal, giving explicit attention to the reciprocating or responding agent even when the response is of no importance to the story line or could be omitted as obvious. The germ of such a tendency may be discerned in the traditional style of alliterative poetry, which provides for the expression of qualities of promptness and readiness in response to commands and requests. . . . But the tendency is sufficiently consistent and systematic in *Gawain* to distinguish that poem from the works of other poets."

19. See Morton W. Bloomfield, "Sir Gawain and the Green Knight: An Appraisal," *PMLA* 76 (1961): 16, 19; Donald R. Howard, *The Three Temptations: Medieval Man in Search of the World* (Princeton, Princeton Univ. Press, 1966), pp. 243–244, 284–285. Bloomfield and Howard principally call attention to the "game" that is the poem, that is, to the game being played by the poet with his audience. J. A. Burrow, *A Reading of Sir Gawain and the Green Knight* (London: Routledge, 1965), pp. 21–23, notes the seriousness, the "vein of legal earnest," with which the Green Knight's Christmas game is taken up. Robert G. Cook, "The Play Element in Sir Gawain and the Green Knight," *Tulane Studies in English* 13 (1963): 5–31, collects the numerous references to and examples of

"play" in the poem itself, with some reference to the ideas of Johan Huizinga's *Homo Ludens* (see note 22 below). Huizinga's ideas have been taken up and applied illuminatingly to medieval drama by V. A. Kolve, *The Play Called Corpus Christi* (Stanford: Stanford Univ. Press, 1966). On "game" in Chaucer, see Richard A. Lanham, "Game, Play, and High Seriousness in Chaucer's Poetry," *English Studies* 48 (1967): 1–24. Huizinga's book founded a whole "anthropology of play." One of its principal documents is Roger Caillois, *Les Jeux et les hommes* (Paris: Gallimard, 1958); see also the issue of *Yale French Studies*, no. 41 (1968), entitled "Game, Play, Literature," and the references in Lanham's article cited above.

20. The precise nature of the game has not been determined. All the elements in the description, vv. 66–70, would be accounted for by a sort of handicapping game (similar to that called "newe faire" in *Piers Plowman*, B V 327 ff.) in which, after New Year's gifts had been exchanged, the giver of the gift judged the less valuable had to make up the difference in kisses.

21. Henry L. Savage, "The Significance of the Hunting Scenes in Sir Gawain and the Green Knight," *JEGP* 27 (1928): 1–15 [repr. in his *The Gawain Poet: Studies in his Personality and Background* (Chapel Hill: Univ. of North Carolina Press, 1956) chap. 2].

22. Johan Huizinga, *Homo Ludens: A Study of the Play-Element in Culture* [1938], Engl. trans. (Boston: Beacon, 1955), p. 45.

23. See vv. 1–5. That it is Aeneas and not Antenor and that Aeneas is meant to be regarded as *trewest on erthe,* despite the *tricherie* attributed to him by medieval tradition, is ably argued, in the context of the whole poem, by Alfred David, "Gawain and Aeneas," *English Studies* 49 (1968): 402–409; cf. also Phillip W. Damon, "Dante's Ulysses and the Mythic Tradition," in William Matthews, ed., *Medieval Secular Literature* (Berkeley, Univ. of California Press, 1965), p. 41.

NOTES TO CHAPTER III

1. See, for instance, the three recent collections of *Piers Plowman* criticism: Robert J. Blanch, ed., *Style and Symbolism in Piers Plowman: A Modern Critical Anthology* (Knox-

ville: Univ. of Tennessee Press, 1969), S. S. Hussey, ed., *Piers Plowman: Critical Approaches*, (London: Methuen, 1969); Edward Vasta, ed., *Interpretations of Piers Plowman* (Notre Dame, Ind.: Univ. of Notre Dame Press, 1968). In my references to the three texts of the poem I shall for convenience use the single edition of Walter W. Skeat, *The Vision of William Concerning Piers the Plowman*, 2 vols. (London: Oxford Univ. Press, 1886; repr. 1954), with some additional punctuation; however, references to the A-text have been checked for meaningful variants against the more authoritative edition of George Kane, *Piers Plowman: the A Version* (London: Univ. of London, the Athlone Press, 1960). My references to events in the poem are to the B-text unless otherwise specified.

2. George Kane, "The Vision of Piers Plowman," in his *Middle English Literature: A Critical Study of the Romances, the Religious Lyrics, Piers Plowman* (London: Methuen, 1951), p. 185; A. C. Spearing, "The Art of Preaching and *Piers Plowman*," in his *Criticism and Medieval Poetry* (New York: Barnes and Noble, 1964), p. 92; Morton Bloomfield, *Piers Plowman as a Fourteenth-century Apocalypse* (New Brunswick, N.J.: Rutgers Univ. Press, 1963), p. 20; John Lawlor, "The Imaginative Unity of Piers Plowman," *Review of English Studies*, n.s., 8 (1957): 126; Elizabeth Salter and Derek Pearsall, eds., *Piers Plowman* (Evanston: Northwestern Univ. Press, 1967), pp. 42, 47.

3. On literary theory see Edmond Faral, ed., *Les Arts poétiques du XIIᵉ et du XIIIᵉ siècle* (Paris: Champion, 1924); on aesthetic theory see Edgar de Bruyne, *Etudes d'esthétique médiévale*, 3 vols. (Bruges: De Tempel, 1946). There is a convenient summary of these subjects in Robert M. Jordan, *Chaucer and the Shape of Creation: The Aesthetic Possibilities of Inorganic Structure* (Cambridge, Mass.: Harvard Univ. Press, 1967), chap. 2. Arthur K. Moore, "Medieval English Literature and the Question of Unity," *Modern Philology* 65 (1968): 285–300, discusses the theoretical and practical difficulties of applying modern conceptions of "unity" to medieval literature; a few pages (289, 294–296) take up *Piers Plowman*.

4. Robert Worth Frank, Jr., *Piers Plowman and the Scheme of Salvation: An Interpretation of Dowel, Dobet and Dobest*, (New Haven: Yale Univ. Press, 1957), p. 34.

5. The principal older theories are summarized by S. S. Hussey, "Langland, Hilton, and the Three Lives," *RES*, n.s.,

7 (1956), pp. 132–150 (repr. Vasta, *Interpretations*, pp. 232–258).

6. See Hussey, "Langland," p. 148 and note; Salter and Pearsall, *Piers*, pp. 29–30.

7. Kane, "Vision," pp. 240–241.

8. Bloomfield, *Piers as Apocalypse*, p. 116.

9. This is the implication of Lawlor, "Imaginative Unity," *passim*, and Spearing, "Art of Preaching," pp. 92–94.

10. *Piers as Apocalypse*, pp. 20–21.

11. Rosemary Woolf, "Some Non-Medieval Qualities of *Piers Plowman*," *Essays in Criticism* 12 (1962): 120.

12. Salter and Pearsall, *Piers*, pp. 8, 42–43.

13. "Vision," p. 244.

14. "Imaginative Unity," pp. 125–126. Lawlor is one of the ablest and most sympathetic readers of the poem. In accepting the poem's incoherencies as part of its artistic plan, he wisely does not insist on its complete artfulness: "We may well, if we choose, identify the poet behind the Dreamer, manoeuvring the reader through his guide until vision is inescapable. But we should be very sure that we allow for the activity of the poem itself, bringing to the poet, in the act of telling, new relations and significances. Our criticism will be beside the mark if we do not see that the poem succeeds in communicating the mind, not behind, but *in* the poem—a poem which is always, in a sense, unfinished." (*Ibid.*) Lawlor's ideas appear in expanded form in his book *Piers Plowman: An Essay in Criticism* (London: Arnold, 1962); see esp, chap. 7.

15. All three texts contain the pairing: AB Prologus 20, 24; C Prologus 22, 25; it is echoed in B XIX 331 (C XXII 337): "Now is Pieres to the plow and Pruyde it aspyde." Kane's edition of the A-text (Prol. 20) offers the reading "to plouz," making "plow" a verb instead of a noun. In either sense, the word comes, of course, with powerful symbolic value in itself, but this does not alter the contrast in concreteness of the paired terms. Another obvious example of the equivalence, in the poet's mind, of terms on different levels of abstraction, comes in the ride to Westminster (Passus II, vv. 161 ff.), where the classes of civil and ecclesiastical officers are mingled freely but not uniformly with moral abstractions. Meed rides on a sheriff; Falsehood on a juryman; Deceit on a flatterer; Simony on the group of summoners and provisors; bishops on deans and other episcopal officers, etc. For further discussion of the mixture of allegory and literalism in Langland, see

Salter and Pearsall, *Piers*, pp. 5, 12, 24; Bloomfield, *Piers as Apocalypse*, pp. 41–42; Lawlor, *Piers*, pp. 252 ff; and Priscilla Jenkins, "Conscience: the Frustration of Allegory," in Hussey, ed., *Piers*, pp. 125–142, where the "interplay between the modes" is provocatively read as "the structural basis of the poem" (p. 125); ". . . allegory is a mode of thought which Langland is investigating and defining through the juxtaposition of allegorical and literal" (p. 142).

16. Raoul de Houdenc, *Le Songe d'Enfer*, in Aug. Scheler, ed., *Trouvères Belges*, Nouvelle Série (Louvain: Lefever, 1879), 2: 176–200.

17. The ensuing two paragraphs repeat observations on Langland's space offered in my "Locus of Action in Medieval Narrative," *Romance Philology* 17 (1963): 115–22, with discussion of space in earlier allegory.

18. Guillaume de Deguileville, *Le Pèlerinage de Vie Humaine*, ed. J. J. Stürzinger (London: Roxburghe Club, 1893), vv. 6503 ff.

19. Spearing, "Art of Preaching," p. 95; cf. Woolf, "Some Non-Medieval Qualities," pp. 114–116.

20. *Piers as Apocalypse*, p. 32; cf. Spearing, "Art of Preaching," p. 87: "one has the impression that the poet is engaged in a contest against an unpredictable opponent."

21. J. F. Goodridge, trans., *Piers the Ploughman* (Harmondsworth: Penguin, 1959), p. 57.

22. See particularly, Spearing, "Art of Preaching," *passim.*

23. See Elizabeth Salter, *Piers Plowman: An Introduction* (Cambridge, Mass.: Harvard Univ. Press, 1962), pp. 24–34; Spearing, "Art of Preaching," pp. 84–89; Salter and Pearsall, *Piers*, pp. 32–35, 48–51, 54. Donald Wesling, "Eschatology and the Language of Satire in 'Piers Plowman," *Criticism* 10 (1968): 287, explains Langland's digressiveness as "unavoidable in the narrative technique of satire."

24. See Lawlor, "Imaginative Unity," pp. 118–119, 124–126; Lawlor, *Piers*, pp. 232–233, 306–316; Salter, *Piers: An Introduction*, pp. 90, 95; Salter and Pearsall, *Piers*, pp. 32, 42–43, 47, 49, 51; Woolf, "Some Non-Medieval Qualities," pp. 120–122; Kane, "Vision," pp. 189–192, 243–245, 247.

25. There is still much to be learned about Langland's poetic style. Perhaps the best brief characterization of the quality of his "making" is Nevill Coghill's "God's Wenches and the Light That Spoke," *English and Medieval Studies Presented to J. R. R. Tolkien*, ed. N. Davis and C. L. Wrenn (London: Allen and Unwin, 1962), pp. 200–218 [repr.

Newstead, *Chaucer and His Contemporaries,* pp. 236–254].
See also Kane, "Vision," *passim;* Elizabeth Suddaby, "The
Poem *Piers Plowman*," *JEGP* 54 (1955): 91–103; Salter,
Piers: An Introduction, pp. 19–24, 31–44; R. E. Kaske, "The
Use of Simple Figures of Speech in *Piers Plowman* B: A
Study in the Figurative Expression of Ideas and Opinions,"
Studies in Philology 48 (1951): 571–600; Lawlor, *Piers,* esp.
pp. 187–280; B. F. Huppé, *"Petrus id est Christus:* Word
Play in Piers Plowman, the B-Text," *ELH* 17 (1950): 163–
190; E. Talbot Donaldson, *Piers Plowman: The C-Text and
Its Poet* (New Haven: Yale Univ. Press, 1949; repr. 1966),
chap. 3.

26. The tradition of the *sermo humilis* is substantially the
discovery of Erich Auerbach; see his *Mimesis,* esp. chaps. 7,
8, and 10; and "Sermo Humilis," in his *Literary Language
and Its Public in Late Latin Antiquity and in the Middle
Ages,* Bollingen Series 74 (New York: Pantheon, 1965), pp.
27–66. Auerbach, however, does not mention *Piers Plowman*
in this connection. The applicability of Auerbach's category
to Langland's plain style has been recently noted by J.A.W.
Bennett, "Chaucer's Contemporary," in Hussey, ed., *Piers,*
p. 316. However, I do not agree that it is equally applicable
to "the rich medley of the *Canterbury Tales.*"

27. "Iurdan" is a pun on "jordan," chamber pot, and
"Jordan," the name of a contemporary friar; on Langland's
general propensity for puns, see Huppé, "Word Play."

28. Lawlor, *Piers,* pp. 262–263; Woolf, "Some Non-
Medieval Qualities," p. 118.

29. Conveniently listed by Huppé, "Word Play," esp. pp.
179 ff. Langland's thematic repetitions, like most repetitions,
at least give the reader a sense of security and familiarity on
the level of ideas. Whether they give the poem structural
coherence is another matter, which cannot at any rate be
proved by the mere listing of them. Some of Langland's
repetitions, as for instance his frequent attacks on the friars,
and his defenses of the poor, seem to work against coherence;
they begin to take on an obsessive quality that threatens interruption of the argument rather than support of it.

30. *Piers as Apocalypse,* pp. 35–36.

31. *Piers: The C-Text,* pp. 78–79. Donaldson continues:
"Knowing A and B, brilliance mingled with mediocrity is just
what we should expect from C."

32. I have not taken up the even more complex question of
a *four*-fold or four-level structure of meaning in *Piers Plow-*

man, in which what I have variously called the allegorical or spiritual significance is further divided into three separate levels of meaning. See D. W. Robertson, Jr., and Bernard F. Huppé, *Piers Plowman and Scriptural Tradition* (Princeton, Princeton Univ. Press, 1951), esp. pp. 2–3, 14, 236–240. According to the present reading of the poem, a four-level edifice is even more likely to have collapsed together in Langland's imagination than a two-level one.

33. I embrace together here the remark by Kane, "Vision," p. 236, that the author has "an unusually powerful visual imagination," and that by Woolf, "Some Non-Medieval Qualities," p. 115, that the poem "lacks the visual quality . . . characteristic of Medieval literature."

34. See in particular, in addition to the works already cited, T. P. Dunning, C.M., *Piers Plowman: An Interpretation of the A Text* (London: Longmans, Green, 1937; excerpts in Vasta, ed., *Interpretations,* pp. 87–114) and his "The Structure of the B-Text of *Piers Plowman,*" *RES,* n.s., 6 (1956): 225–237 (repr. in Vasta, ed., *Interpretations,* pp. 259–277, and in Blanch, ed., *Style and Symbolism,* pp. 87–100); and Sister Mary Clemente Davlin, O.P., "Kynde Knowyng as a Major Theme in *Piers Plowman* B," *RES,* n.s., 22 (1971): 1–19.

35. Robertson and Huppé, *Piers,* p. 236.

36. See Salter, *Piers,* pp. 71–72; Salter and Pearsall, *Piers,* pp. 22–23. That segment of medieval "surrealism" which borders on the grotesque is taken up by Jurgis Baltrušaitis, *Réveils et prodigues: le gothique fantastique* (Paris: Colin, 1960).

37. Millard Meiss, *Painting in Florence and Siena after the Black Death* (Princeton: Princeton Univ. Press, 1951), pp. 25, 93.

NOTES TO CHAPTER IV

1. See chap. I above, pp. 31–32 and footnote 32. For the text of Chaucer, I use *The Works of Geoffrey Chaucer,* ed. F. N. Robinson, 2d ed. (Boston: Houghton Mifflin, 1957).

2. This idea is discussed in some detail in my *"The Canterbury Tales:* Style of the Man and Style of the Work," in D. S. Brewer, ed., *Chaucer and Chaucerians: Critical*

Studies in Middle English Literature (London: Nelson, 1966), pp. 88–114.

3. This is the import of recent "exegetical" criticism; see, for instance, D. W. Robertson, Jr., *A Preface to Chaucer: Studies in Medieval Perspectives* (Princeton: Princeton Univ. Press, 1962), pp. 317–331, 380–382.

4. Ernest Langlois, ed., *Le Roman de la Rose par Guillaume de Lorris et Jean de Meun,* Société des Anciens Textes Français, 5 vols. (Paris: Champion, 1914–1924), vv. 11969–974:

> "Mais a vous n'ose je mentir;
> Mis se je peüsse sentir
> Que vous ne l'aperceüssiez,
> La mençonge ou poing eüssiez:
> Certainement je vous boulasse,
> Ja pour pechié ne la laissasse. . . ."

The Middle English translation (Robinson, ed., *Chaucer,* p. 633), vv. 7287–7292:

> "But unto you dar I not lye;
> But myght I felen or aspie
> That ye perceyved it no thyng,
> Ye shulde have a stark lesyng
> Right in youre honde thus, to bigynne;
> I nolde it lette for no synne."

5. See Erich Auerbach, "Camilla, or, the Rebirth of the Sublime," in his *Literary Language and Its Public,* trans. Ralph Manheim, Bollingen Series 74 (New York: Pantheon, 1965), pp. 183–233. Auerbach discusses the reasons for the decline of the sublime style and describes the steps leading to Dante's full revival of it in the *Divine Comedy.*

6. Robert Kilburn Root, ed., *The Book of Troilus and Criseyde* by Geoffrey Chaucer (Princeton: Princeton Univ. Press, 1926 [repr. 1945]), p. xlv. Cf. Daniel C. Boughner, "Elements of Epic Grandeur in the 'Troilus,' " *ELH* 6 (1939): 200–210; and Paul M. Clogan, "Chaucer's Use of the 'Thebaid,' " *English Miscellany* 18 (1967): 9–31. The best study of the *Teseida's* influence on Chaucer's epic style is R. A. Pratt, "Chaucer's Use of the *Teseida,*" *PMLA* 62 (1947): 598–621. Pratt suggests (p. 612) that the example of the *Teseida* "may have had more to do with Chaucer's decision to rework the story of *Il Filostrato* in a heightened manner than the example of Dante's *Commedia.* . . ."

7. Giovanni Boccaccio, *Teseida delle nozze d'Emilia,* ed. Aurelio Roncaglia (Bari: Laterza, 1941), XII, 84; cf. Boccaccio's *chiose* to XII, 84 and 85, p. 465. Boccaccio is referring to *De Vulgari eloquentia* II, ii, 8: "Quare hec tria, salus videlicet, venus et virtus, apparent esse illa magnalia que sint maxime pertractanda, hoc est ea que maxime sunt ad ista, ut armorum probitas, amoris accensio et directio voluntatis" (ed. A. Marigo, 3d ed. [Firenze: Le Monnier, 1957]).

8. See Robert S. Haller, *"The Knight's Tale* and the Epic Tradition," *Chaucer Review* 1 (1966): 67–84; dealing mainly with the ethical and political import of epic, Professor Haller argues persuasively that "it is in his treatment of love that Chaucer is most epic, for what Chaucer has done is to make love take the place of the usual political center of the epic . . ."; love is "the means whereby the cosmic and political implications of the epic are conveyed" (p. 68).

9. See Derek Pearsall, "The Squire as Story-Teller," *UTQ* 34 (1965): 82–92; Robert S. Haller, "Chaucer's *Squire's Tale* and the Uses of Rhetoric," *Modern Philology* 62 (1965): 285–295.

10. Brian Wilkie, "What is Sentimentality?," *College English* 28 (1967): 564–575, is an excellent statement of the problem.

11. Medieval romance contains from the first an "Ovidian" strain of pathos having to do with unhappy heroines, but it is rarely so overstated as to approach sentimentality. Mr. Richard Lock has pointed out to me a rare instance (and the earliest I know) of the introduction of a child for pathetic effect in romance: *The Continuations of the Old French Perceval of Chrétien de Troyes,* vol. I, *The First Continuation,* ed. William Roach (Philadelphia: Univ. of Pennsylvania Press, 1949), vv. 10857–10948, 11035–11079.

12. On Mâle, see above, chap. I and notes 22 & 23. The very popular *Meditations on the Life of Christ,* written probably first in Latin by a Franciscan living in Tuscany in the second half of the thirteenth century, still exists in over two hundred manuscripts in various languages. See *Meditations on the Life of Christ,* ed. and trans. Isa Ragusa and Rosalie B. Green (Princeton: Princeton Univ. Press, 1961), a modern English translation based mainly on an Italian version. The *Meditations* were translated into English in the fifteenth century by Nicholas Love; see Elizabeth Zeeman, "Nicholas Love—A Fifteenth-Century Translator," *RES,* n.s., 6 (1955): 113–127. In the same approximate period as the

pseudo-Bonaventura, or slightly earlier, is the *Legenda Aurea* (ca. 1255) of Jacobus de Varagine, with quite a few saints' legends containing pathetic incidents.

13. Treatment of mothers and children in a pathetic vein are rare in English literature between Chaucer and the eighteenth century. Addison's *Spectator* paper no. 44 (April 20, 1711) signals the change of taste: "A disconsolate Mother, with a Child in her Hand, has frequently drawn Compassion from the Audience, and has therefore gained a Place in several Tragedies. A Modern Writer, that observed how this had took in other Plays, being resolved to double the Distress, and melt his Audience twice as much as those before him had done, brought a Princess upon the Stage with a little Boy in one Hand and a Girl in the other. . . ." (ed. G. Gregory Smith, vol. 1, Everyman's Library, no. 164 [London: Dent, 1945], p. 133.)

14. See William S. Wilson, "Exegetical Grammar in the *House of Fame*," *English Language Notes* 1 (1964): 246.

15. Johan Huizinga, *Waning of the Middle Ages* [1919; Eng. trans. 1924] (London: Arnold, 1937), pp. 126–128.

16. The thirteenth has been called "the century of the discovery of childhood." See Philippe Ariès, *Centuries of Childhood: A Social History of Family Life,* trans. Robert Baldick (New York: Knopf, 1962), esp. pp. 33–49, "The Discovery of Childhood;" E. Delaruelle, "L'Idée de croisade chez Saint Louis," *Bulletin de Littérature Ecclésiastique* 61 (1960): 252. I have been unable to obtain the 36-page work cited by both: Pierre Colombier, *L'Enfant au Moyen Age* (Villefranche-sur-Rhône: Jacquemaire, 1951).

17. D. S. Brewer, "Children in Chaucer," *Review of English Literature* 5 (1964): 55–56.

18. Quoted in Erich Auerbach, *Mimesis: The Representation of Reality in Western Literature* [1946], trans. Willard R. Trask (Princeton: Princeton Univ. Press, 1953), p. 239.

19. Theodore Spencer, "The Story of Ugolino in Dante and Chaucer," *Speculum* 9 (1934): 295–301.

20. See, for flaccid narration, 105 ff.; 155–157, 174, 217; and for vague plot, 139 ff., 260 ff.

21. The "soft" view of the tale, accepting its pathos fully, is the traditional view, dominant until recent times; for an excellent presentation of the "hard" view, see Alan T. Gaylord, "The Unconquered Tale of the Prioress," *Papers of the Michigan Academy of Science, Arts, and Letters* 47 (1962): 613–636.

22. This argument is elaborated in my *Chaucer and the French Tradition: A Study in Style and Meaning* (Berkeley: Univ. of California Press, 1957), pp. 190–197.

23. Alfred David, "The Man of Law vs. Chaucer: A Case in Poetics," *PMLA* 82 (1967): 223.

24. See, e.g., vv. 267–273, 295–315, 358–371, 421–427, 470–504, 631–637, 652–658, etc.

25. Frederick A. Pottle, *The Idiom of Poetry* (Ithaca, Cornell Univ. Press, 1941), p. 32: "Poetry in the bulk, poetry by and large, infallibly expresses the sensibility of the age which produced it. If it did not, it would not be poetry at all. And hence I say that poetry, in the collective sense, cannot go wrong."

INDEX

ABC, 113, 130, 135
Addison, J., 163
Aeneid, 120, 121
Ammianus Marcellinus, 12, 13
Anderson, J. J., 151
Anelida and Arcite, 118, 122, 123, 128
Anselm of Canterbury, 129
Antoine de la Sale, 136
Ariès, P., 163
Ariosto, 119
Auerbach, E., 8–10, 11, 12–13, 147, 159, 161, 163

Bailey, R. W., 147
Baldick, R., 163
Ball, J., 17, 18, 20
Baltrušaitis, J., 160
Bennett, J. A. W., 159
Benson, L. D., 153
Bernard of Clairvaux, 129
Berry, F., 154
Bessinger, J. B., Jr., 154
Blanche, Duchess of Lancaster, 27, 114
Blanch, R. J., 152, 153, 155, 160
Bloomfield, M., 72, 78, 89, 105, 151, 154, 156, 157
Boccaccio, 119, 121, 162
Boethius, 31
Bonaventura (pseudo-), 129, 163
Book of the Duchess, 27, 114, 119
Borroff, M., 61, 153, 154
Bosch, H., 108
Boughner, D. C., 161

Brewer, D. S., 136, 152, 160, 163
Bright, W., 147
Brooks, C., 10
Brown, C., 40, 152
Burrow, J. A., 154
Burton, D. M., 147

Caillois, R., 155
Canterbury Tales, 29, 30, 74, 111, 112, 125, 126, 130, 144, 159. *See also individual titles*
Cantor, N. E., 147
Cawley, A. C., 153
Chatman, S., 147
Chaucer, G., 14, 18, 19, 24, 25, 26–35, 71, 93, 108, 111–144, 160 (ed.), 161, 162, 163. *See also individual works*
Chaumpaigne, C., 30
Chrétien de Troyes, 119
Cleanness (Purity), 34, 37, 39, 151 (ed.)
Clerk's Tale, 130, 135, 140, 141, 142
Clogan, P. M., 161
Coghill, N., 158
Colombier, P., 163
Consolation of Philosophy, 31, 76, 142
Cook, R. G., 154
Cox, H., 154
Crow, M. M., 150

Daedalus, 146
Damon, P. W., 155

Dante, 9, 42, 84, 88, 94, 119,
    120, 121, 161. *See also indi-
    vidual works*
David, A., 142, 155, 164
Davis, N., 151, 158
Davlin, Sister M. C., 160
De Bello Troiano, 119
De Bruyne, E., 156
Decameron, 74
De contemptu mundi, 142
Deguileville, G. de, 130, 158.
    See also Pèlerinage
Delaruelle, E., 163
Deschamps, E., 24, 25, 119
De Vulgari eloquentia, 120, 162
Divine Comedy, 7, 8, 42, 74,
    120, 161
Dobson, R. B., 148, 149
Donaldson, E. T., Jr., 29, 105,
    150, 159
DuBoulay, F. R. H., 148
Dunning, T. P., 160
Dvořák, M., 7

Edward II, 19
Edward III, 19, 26, 83
Evans, J., 149
Everett, D., 153

Faral, E., 156
Ford, B., 154
Fouquet, J., 24
Franklin's Tale, 118, 127
Frank, R. W., Jr., 156
Freeman, D. C., 147
Froissart, J., 24, 119
Fryde, E. B., 148

Gaylord, A. T., 163
*General Prologue, Canterbury
    Tales,* 112
Gerber, J., 146
Giotto, 108
Goldhurst, W., 154

Gombrich, E. H., 147
Goodridge, J. F., 158
Gordon, E. V., 151, 152
Gower, J., 24
Green, R. B., 162
Guillaume de Deguileville, 130,
    158. *See also Pèlerinage*
Guillaume de Lorris, 119

Haller, R. S., 162
Heers, J., 148
Henry IV, 27
Herbert, G., 69
Hopkins, G. M., 69
Houdenc, R. de, 158
House of Fame, 27, 108, 111,
    112, 114, 120–121, 126–127,
    128, 131, 141
Howard, D. R., 53, 154
Huizinga, J., 14, 25, 68, 135,
    147, 150, 155, 163
Huppé, B. F., 159, 160
Hussey, S. S., 156, 157, 158,
    159

Il Filostrato, 161
Inferno, 88, 137

Jacobus de Varagine, 163
Jenkins, P., 158
John of Gaunt, 18, 21, 26, 27,
    30
Johnson, W. S., 41, 48, 152,
    153
Jones, R. H., 149
Jordan, R. M., 156
Joseph of Exeter, 119
Joyce, J., 69

Kane, G., 33, 72, 79, 151, 156,
    157, 158, 159, 160
Kaske, R. E., 159
Kean, P. M., 152, 153
Kempe, M., 149

Kent, J., 30
Kittredge, G. L., 29, 150
Knight's Tale, 118, 122–123, 125–126, 134, 138, 162
Kolve, V. A., 155

Langland, W., 14, 25, 33, 34, 71–109, 112, 157, 158, 159, 160. *See also Piers Plowman*
Langlois, E., 161
Lanham, R. A., 155
Lawlor, J., 72, 80, 105, 152, 156, 157, 158, 159
Leff, G., 22, 149
Legenda Aurea, 163
Legend of Good Women, 118, 121, 122, 128, 132
Lerner, R. E., 147
Levin, S., 147
Lewis, R. W. B., 6
Lock, R., 162
Lorris, Guillaume de, 119
Love, N., 162
Luttrell, C. A., 153

Machaut, G., 24, 119
McKisack, M., 19, 148
Mâle, E., 23, 24, 149, 150, 162
Manheim, R., 147, 161
Man of Law's Tale, 135, 141–142
Marigo, A., 162
Marx, L., 6, 146
Mathew, G., 19, 149
Matthews, W., 155
Meditations on the Life of Christ, 129, 162
Meiss, M., 108, 160
Menner, R. J., 151
Milton, J., 119
Moore, A. K., 156
Morse, J. M., 146
Muscatine, C., 151, 158, 160, 164

Myers, A. R., 149

New Literary History, 147
Newstead, H., 152, 159
Nun's Priest's Tale, 28, 108, 113

Ohmann, R., 147
Olson, C. C., 150
Oman, C., 148
Orcagna, 108
Owl and the Nightingale, 76

Palmer, J. J. N., 151
Pantin, W. A., 149
Paradise Lost, 7
Pardoner's Tale, 116, 135
Parliament of Fowls, 27, 114
Patience, 34, 38, 41, 151 (ed.)
Pearce, R. H., 4, 6, 146
Pearl, 34, 35, 40–55, 56, 60, 68, 71, 76, 108, 151 (ed.)
Pearl poet, 14, 25, 37–69, 71, 111, 151. *See also individual works*
Pearsall, D., 72, 79, 156, 157, 158, 162
Pèlerinage de Vie Humaine, 87, 158 (ed.)
Perceval, Continuations, 162
Phillips, C., 1
Physician's Tale, 135, 138, 139
Piers Plowman, 33, 39, 71–109, 111, 151, 155, 156 (ed.), 159. *See also Langland*
Pottle, F. A., 144, 164
Prioress's Tale, 135, 139–140, 141, 142
Purity, 34, 37, 39, 151 (ed.)

Ragusa, I., 162
Randall, D. B. J., 153
Raoul de Houdenc, 158
Réconfort de Madame du Fresne, 136

Retractation, 113
Richard II, 18, 19, 22, 27
Rickert, M., 149
Roach, W., 162
Robertson, D. W., Jr., 160, 161
Robinson, F. N., 160, 161
Roman de la Rose, 76, 117
Romano, R., 148
Roncaglia, A., 162
Root, R. K., 119, 120, 161
Russell, J. B., 148

St. Erkenwald, 34
Sallust, 12
Salter, E., 72, 79, 155, 156, 157, 158, 159, 160. *See also Zeeman*
Savage, H. L., 65
Scheler, A., 158
Second Nun's Tale, 131, 135
Siciliano, I., 150
Sir Gawain and the Green Knight, 34, 35, 41–45, 51, 55–69, 71, 108, 125, 151 (ed.)
Skeat, W. W., 156
Smith, G. G., 163
Smith, H. N., 6
Songe d'Enfer, 83, 158
Spearing, A. C., 72, 152, 153, 156, 157, 158
Spectator, 163
Spencer, T., 137, 163
Spitzer, L., 8, 11, 147
Squire's Tale, 127–128
Statius, 119, 122, 161
Steel, A., 149
Stevens, W., 69
Stürzinger, J. J., 158
Sudbury, S., 18
Suddaby, E., 159
Swynford, K., 26

Tacitus, 12, 13

Tasso, T., 119
Tatlock, J. S. P., 150
Taylor, P. B., 154
Tenenti, A., 148
Teseida, 120, 122, 161, 162
Thebaid, 122, 161
Tolkien, J. R. R., 151
Trask, W. R., 147, 163
Troilus and Criseyde, 32, 111, 113, 115, 118, 123–125, 126, 138, 144

Van Eyck, J., 24
Vasta, E., 152, 156, 157, 160
Vergil, 119, 120, 121
Villon, F., 25

Walsingham, T., 17, 18, 20
Ward, J. W., 6
Ward, L. L., 1
Warren, A., 146, 147
Warren, R. P., 10
Weimann, R., 146
Wellek, R., 146, 147, 152
Wesling, D., 158
Wife of Bath's Prologue, 115
Wife of Bath's Tale, 127
Wilkie, B., 162
Williams, E. C., 150
Wilson, W. S., 163
Wimsatt, W. K., Jr., 10
Wölfflin, H., 7
Woolf, R., 78, 105, 157, 158, 159, 160
Wordsworth, W., *Prelude,* 33
Worringer, W., 7
Wrawe, J., 20
Wrenn, C. L., 158
Wyclif, J., 21, 30

Yale French Studies, 155

Zeeman (Salter), E., 162